Foundations of ENGLISH
GUIDED NOTEBOOK

Editors: Caitlin Clark, Katherine Cleveland, Caitlin Edahl, Sarah Quinn

Designers: James Smalls, Patrick Thompson, Tee Jay Zajac
Cover Design: James Smalls

VP Research & Development: Marcel Prevuznak

A division of Quant Systems, Inc.

546 Long Point Road, Mount Pleasant, SC 29464

Copyright © 2018 by Hawkes Learning/Quant Systems, Inc. All rights reserved.

No part of this publication may be reproduced, stored in a retrieval system, or transmitted in any form or by any means, electronic, mechanical, photocopying, recording, or otherwise, without the prior written consent of the publisher.

Printed in the United States of America

10 9 8 7 6 5 4 3

ISBN: 978-1-946158-86-4

Table of Contents

Chapter 1

Study Skills

1.1	Understanding Different Learning Styles	1
1.2	Determining Your Personal Learning Style	4
1.3	Understanding and Reducing Stress	9
1.4	Keeping Yourself Organized	13
1.5	Managing Your Time Effectively	16
1.6	Taking Notes and Annotating Texts	23
1.7	Using Effective Study Strategies	27
1.8	Reducing Test Anxiety	30
1.9	Taking Advantage of Campus Resources	32

Chapter 2

Reading Skills

2.1	Preparing Yourself to Read	35
2.2	Using Visual Clues	39
2.3	Reading Actively and Purposefully	42
2.4	Deconstructing Topics, Ideas, and Details	45
2.5	Identifying Organizational Patterns	49
2.6	Using Context for Unfamiliar Words or Phrases	54
2.7	Using Word Parts for Unfamiliar Phrases	58
2.8	Making Inferences about a Text	61
2.9	Recognizing Types of Main Ideas and Evidence	64

Chapter 3

Critical Thinking

3.1	Identifying Purpose and Tone	69
3.2	Analyzing Argumentation Strategies	74
3.3	Identifying Bias	78
3.4	Evaluating Evidence	82
3.5	Understanding the Basics of Logic	85
3.6	Recognizing Logical Fallacies	89
3.7	Analyzing and Evaluating Visuals	93

Chapter 4

Grammar and Mechanics

4.1	Understanding Nouns	97
4.2	Understanding Pronouns	102
4.3	Understanding Verbs	109
4.4	Understanding Adjectives and Adverbs	118
4.5	Understanding Prepositions	121
4.6	Understanding Clauses and Conjunctions	124
4.7	Identifying the Characteristics of Sentences	130
4.8	Identifying Common Sentence Errors	138
4.9	Using Consistent Subjects and Verbs	142
4.10	Using Consistent Pronouns and Antecedents	146
4.11	Using Correct Pronoun Reference and Case	149
4.12	Using Commas	153
4.13	Using Semicolons and Colons	157
4.14	Using Apostrophes	160
4.15	Using Quotation Marks, Parentheses, and Brackets	163
4.16	Using Ellipses, Hyphens, and Dashes	165
4.17	Using Capitalization and Italics	168
4.18	Using Abbreviations and Numbers	171
4.19	Using Basic Spelling Rules	173
4.20	Spelling Commonly Confused Words	179
4.21	Proofreading Sentences for Grammar	183

Chapter 5

Style

5.1	Determining a Writing Style	191
5.2	Using an Appropriate Tone	195
5.3	Maintaining Consistency in Tense and Person	198
5.4	Correcting Misplaced and Dangling Modifiers	202
5.5	Using Word and Sentence Variety	204
5.6	Using Parallelism, Coordination, and Subordination	208
5.7	Using Active and Passive Voice	210
5.8	Emphasizing Words or Phrases	212
5.9	Choosing Clear, Concise, and Vivid Words	214
5.10	Using Inclusive Language	217
5.11	Proofreading Sentences for Style	219

Chapter 6

Writing Paragraphs

6.1	The Writing Process for Paragraphs	221
6.2	Choosing a Topic and Scope for a Paragraph	226
6.3	Writing a Topic Sentence	232
6.4	Choosing an Organizational Pattern	235
6.5	Drafting a Paragraph	240
6.6	Revising and Editing a Paragraph	244
6.7	Submitting a Paragraph	247

Chapter 7

Writing Longer Texts

7.1	Preparing to Write a Longer Text	249
7.2	Understanding Genre and Purpose	252
7.3	Choosing a Topic and Scope for a Longer Text	256
7.4	Writing a Thesis or Purpose Statement	259
7.5	Organizing and Outlining a Paper	262
7.6	Writing with Technology	265
7.7	Writing a First Draft	267
7.8	Using Paragraphs Effectively	269
7.9	Revising a Longer Text	273
7.10	Participating in Peer Review	275
7.11	Submitting a Longer Text	278

Chapter 8

Research

8.1	Researching and Writing Responsibly	281
8.2	Making a Research Plan	288
8.3	Organizing the Research Process	291
8.4	Identifying Types of Sources	294
8.5	Evaluating the Credibility of Sources	297
8.6	Applying MLA Styles and Formatting	300

Chapter 1
Study Skills

Lesson 1.1
Understanding Different Learning Styles

OBJECTIVE

★ Recognize the characteristics of the eight learning styles.

BIG IDEA

Everyone understands and processes information in different ways. Researchers Richard Felder and Linda K. Silverman have organized learning styles into four pairs:

1.   3.

2.   4.

In this lesson, you will learn about the following learning styles:

- Visual and Verbal Learning
- Active and Reflective Learning
- Sensing and Intuitive Learning
- Sequential and Global Learning

Visual and Verbal Learning

Visual learners use _____ to learn new concepts. _____, _____, and _____ are much more memorable to visual learners than are words.

List four resources that visual learners might find most useful:

1.   3.

2.   4.

Verbal learners understand information from _____. These learners are usually good at remembering what people said, but they may _____ to remember what people _____ _____.

Lesson 1.1 | Understanding Different Learning Styles

List five resources that verbal learners might find most useful:

1.
2.
5.

3.
4.

Active and Reflective Learning

Active learners like to be _____.

Active learners enjoy lively _____ _____ or _____ _____.

Reflective learners like to _____ on new _____ by themselves.

Define the term **reflective**.

Which type of learner:
- enjoys working with friends on projects?
- might consider himself a hands-on learner?
- sometimes finds herself procrastinating on big projects?
- sometimes practices important conversations in his head?
- is good at figuring things out on her own?

Sensing and Intuitive Learning

The word *sensing* is related to your five _____.

Sensing learners like to solve problems through methods that are _____ and _____. They are the most comfortable with objective facts and don't like surprises.

The word *intuitive* comes from the word _____, which means knowing something by _____ or "_____ _____."

Sequential and Global Learning

Sequential learners prefer to learn information in a _____ _____.

Explain the meaning of *linear*.

Global learners like to understand the _____-_____ _____ ideas first.

Which type of learner:
- might say "I'll come back to that later?"
- prefers to learn something in sequential order?
- may feel overwhelmed by a project unless it's been broken down into orderly tasks?
- might store up knowledge until suddenly everything fits together and makes sense?
- might want someone to describe the big picture for him or her?

Lesson Wrap-up

Key Terms

Define the following Key Terms from this lesson.

Active Learning:

Global Learning:

Intuitive Learning:

Learning Style:

Reflective Learning:

Sensing Learning:

Sequential Learning:

Verbal Learning:

Visual Learning:

Lesson 1.2
Determining Your Personal Learning Styles

OBJECTIVES

★ Apply an understanding of learning styles to real-life situations.
★ Create success strategies for different types of learning.

BIG IDEA

Knowing your own personal learning styles can help you overcome any frustration you feel when learning new information.

List the eight different types of learning styles:

1.   5.

2.   6.

3.   7.

4.   8.

In this lesson, you will learn about the following:

- Exploring Your Personal Learning Styles
- Learning Style Strategies
- Learning Styles Outside of School

Exploring Your Personal Learning Styles

To find your personal learning styles, you need to think about your _____ learning experiences and _____ _____.

Read through the student profiles in the text carefully. Then, for each pair, write which profile seems to describe you best; write *both* if both profiles fit you equally.

- Visual Learner, Verbal Learner, or both?

- Active Learner, Reflective Learner, or both?

- Sensing Learner, Intuitive Learner, or both?

- Sequential Learner, Global Learner, or both?

Learning Style Strategies

Visual and Verbal Learning

If you're a visual learner, you should use more _____, _____, or _____ during your study time.

- _____ of people or events with photos from Google image search (https://www.google.com/imghp) or Wikimedia Commons (https://commons.wikimedia.org/wiki/Main_Page). Be sure to include any important names, facts, or dates next to each photo.

- _____ _____ or _____ to color-code your class notes. For example, key terms could be highlighted blue while important names could be highlighted pink.

- _____ a YouTube (https://www.youtube.com) video about the topic. If you find a helpful video, consider sharing it with the rest of your class.

If you're a verbal learner, look for opportunities to study with _____ or _____ recordings.

- _____ or _____ a summary of class lectures and readings. You can use a notebook to keep hand-written notes organized or Google Docs (https://accounts.google.com/) to keep digital documents organized and up-to-date.

- _____ to an audiobook while you're reading. Project Gutenberg (http://www.gutenberg.org/wiki/Gutenberg:The_Audio_Books_Project) has a collection of free classics, and the local library has modern titles to checkout or download.

- With your instructor permission, _____ class lectures and listen to them at home. If you don't have an audio recorder, you can usually borrow one from the campus library.

Active and Reflective Learning

If you're an active learner, you like to turn _____ into _____.

- _____ with a group of classmates for a study group. Assign a section of information to each group member and take turns teaching your topics to the rest of the group.

- Make your own practice _____ and review _____. You can use index cards or a website like Quizlet (http://quizlet.com/) to test yourself.

- _____ while you're studying. Stretching your legs and getting a breath of fresh air can help you stay focused on less active tasks.

Lesson 1.2 | Determining Your Personal Learning Styles

If you're a reflective learner, you usually spend time _____ about an idea before _____ on it.

- Find a quiet _____ that's free from distractions. You can try using a white noise website like RainyMood (www.rainymood.com/) to block out noisy family members or roommates.

- Use a _____ to save class notes and returned tests to review later. If you review them during class, don't be afraid to write down any corrected answers or notes.

- Use a _____ or _____ _____ like Evernote (https://evernote.com/) to journal your thoughts about what you learned in class and how you can apply this to the world around you. Read back through your journal entries while you're preparing for class.

Sensing and Intuitive Learning

If you're a sensing learner, you feel the most comfortable learning _____ facts and applying those facts to the _____ world.

- _____ how a topic is used in real-life situations. Don't be afraid to talk with your instructor about how the information could apply to different professions.

- _____ a site like Pinterest (http://www.pinterest.com) to start a collection of helpful study tips or project ideas. Just don't let yourself get distracted by double-chocolate caramel brownie recipes!

- _____ with a study group to discuss the *why* behind facts. Talking to people with different points of view can help you understand all sides of a topic.

If you're an intuitive learner, you enjoy thinking _____.

- _____. Sometimes a new location can help inspire you with new ideas.

- _____ while studying "boring" subjects. You can use an app like Spotify (https://www.spotify.com/) to make yourself a custom study playlist.

- _____ to keep assignments organized. An online resource like Google Calendar allows you to plan your schedule and set reminders for important tasks.

Sequential Learning and Global Learning

If you're a sequential learner, you learn information in _____, _____ steps.

- _____ of key ideas from class readings. Then, arrange this information into an outline or bullet list that you can use to study later.

- _____ on a site like WikiHow (http://www.wikihow.com/). You could even consider writing your own step-by-step directions to help you think through the entire process.

- _____ for large projects. You can print paper checklists or use an app like Wunderlist (https://www.wunderlist.com/) to keep a digital list.

If you're a <u>global</u> learner, you learn information in _____ bursts of understanding and like to look at the _____ _____ first.

- _____ the table of contents or section headings before starting a reading. Use this information to get a better idea of how the different chapters or sections fit together.
- _____ to show how smaller ideas are connected to the main idea. Programs like Microsoft Word or PowerPoint have built-in tools to create flowcharts, cluster diagrams, and idea trees.
- _____ before starting a new reading or project. Even though it's not a reliable source for academic papers or presentations, Wikipedia (http://wikipedia.org) can be a great place to read an overview of a topic.

Learning Styles Outside of School

You can use the same learning styles strategies to help you find success at _____ or in your _____ life.

Knowing your learning styles can help you determine exactly which _____ or _____ is going to make the most sense to you.

Lesson Wrap-up

Test Yourself

Next to each statement, write **T** for True or **F** for False. Check your work using the Answer Key in the back of the book.

1. _____ Knowing your individual learning style(s) can help you find success at work or in your personal life.
2. _____ You should not let your instructor know that you might need the information explained in a different way.
3. _____ Learning styles should never be an excuse for bad study habits.
4. _____ Most instructors would be happy to meet with you if you explain you're having some difficulty with the class and you'd like to become a better student.
5. _____ An instructor would not want you to use any other resources besides the textbook and notes for his/her class.

6. _____ Many people are either visual learners or verbal learners, and it is best if they limit themselves to just visuals or plain text.

7. _____ Using a balance of your learning styles will help you make the most of your study time.

8. _____ Global learners can use their knowledge of the big picture to understand smaller details.

9. _____ Learning styles are helpful only for academic purposes.

Choose the best term and fill in the blank. Check your work using the Answer Key in the back of the book.

10. Which kind of learner might act a little too quickly and then not understand the information? (*reflective* or *active*) _____

11. Which kind of learner enjoys thinking creatively? (*sensing* or *intuitive*) _____

12. Which kind of learner might say, "I need a smaller, more manageable task"? (*sequential* or *global*) _____

Key Terms

Define the following Key Terms from this lesson.

Active Learning:

Global Learning:

Intuitive Learning:

Learning Style:

Planner:

Reflective Learning:

Sensing Learning:

Sequential Learning:

Verbal Learning:

Visual Learning:

Workspace:

Lesson 1.3
Understanding and Reducing Stress

OBJECTIVES

★ Learn basic stress-management strategies.
★ Understand the causes of stress.

BIG IDEA

Stress can't always be avoided completely, but strategies for keeping it under control can reduce your likelihood of becoming overwhelmed.

In this lesson, you will learn three ways to manage your stress more effectively:

- Determine Causes of Stress
- Put Everything into Perspective
- Make a Plan to Move Forward

Determine Causes of Stress

Define the term **external stress**.

Define the term **internal stress**.

Read the three scenarios in the lesson about Jordan, Kimani, and Layla who are all experiencing stress. Make a list of the **internal** and **external** factors causing stress in these situations. Write your list in the table below.

Student	Internal Stress	External Stress
Jordan		
Kimani		
Layla		

Lesson 1.3 | Understanding and Reducing Stress

On Your Own

Think through the causes of your own stress and write them in the table below. Make sure to consider both external and internal sources.

External Causes	Internal Causes

Put Everything into Perspective

Sometimes, when you're feeling stressed, every task seems equally _____ and _____. If you step back and re-evaluate, however, you'll probably find that not everything is as big as you thought.

Take the time to think through each situation _____ and ask yourself some of the following questions:

1.
2.
3.

On Your Own

Prioritize your own stress in the table below.

Stress	Rank	Reason

Make a Plan to Move Forward

Once you've identified the _____ of your stress and put them into _____, you can begin finding ways to deal with them. To manage your stress more _____, try some of these strategies:

Write a brief definition for each stress-management strategy.

1. Take action:

2. Keep yourself organized:

3. Don't be afraid to ask for help:

4. Relax and recharge:

5. Prevent stress before it starts:

Lesson Wrap-up

Test Yourself

Next to each statement, write **T** for True or **F** for False. Check your work using the Answer Key in the back of the book.

1. _____ You should never feel stress at school; if you do, you're probably doing something wrong.
2. _____ The first step in managing your stress is to determine what's causing it.
3. _____ Procrastination means to get your priorities right.
4. _____ It's best to procrastinate when planning when to study.
5. _____ Planning and organizing are the opposite of procrastinating.
6. _____ Taking action to manage your stress might mean that you will make a to-do list and place the most important tasks at the top.
7. _____ The Student Services Office at your school is a good place to seek out help if you need counseling or tutoring services.

Lesson 1.3 | Understanding and Reducing Stress

Choose the best answer and fill in the blank. Check your work using the Answer Key in the back of the book.

8. A student who has three tests in one day is experiencing which kind of stress? (*internal* or *external*)

   _____

9. A student who's worried about a science exam because someone told her that the professor demands perfection would be experiencing which kind of stress? (*internal* or *external*)

   _____

10. Which of the following would be your top priority? (*your semester final exam next week* or *a class project due in November*) _____

Key Terms

Define the following Key Terms from this lesson.

External Stress:

Internal Conflict:

Student Services:

Lesson 1.4
Keeping Yourself Organized

OBJECTIVE

★ Learn basic organization strategies.

BIG IDEA

Staying on top of your responsibilities is much easier when you have a structured plan for keeping everything organized.

This lesson will discuss three helpful ways to keep yourself organized and on track:
- Keep a Planner
- Use a File System
- Create a Workspace

Keep a Planner

A **planner** is a place for you to organize your _____ and record any _____ _____ or _____.

Before filling out your _____, gather everything with important _____ and deadlines, including any course syllabi. These documents include class _____, major project _____, and assignment _____ dates.

You should also gather the following items:

- _____
- _____
- _____
- _____
- _____

Explain the top-down strategy:

Checklist: Filling in a Student Planner

What three steps should you take when recording events in your planner?

✓

✓

✓

Lesson 1.4 | Keeping Yourself Organized

Define the term **digital planner**.

Use a File System

Why is it a good idea to save class papers?

The first step in staying organized is knowing _____ to save.

The second step in staying organized is deciding _____ to save everything.

You should keep a separate folder for each of your _____ and _____.

Creating a Workspace

An organized **workspace** is essential for working _____.

Describe your ideal workspace for studying:

Why do you think it is important to keep your workspace free of clutter?

What are some of the materials you should have at your workspace?

On Your Own

To think through your own study habits, answer the following questions:
- Do you prefer studying in the morning or evening?
- When you study, do you prefer silence or noise?
- Would you rather study inside or outside?
- Do you prefer studying alone or in a group?

Lesson Wrap-up

Test Yourself

Next to each statement, write **T** for True or **F** for False. Check your work using the Answer Key in the back of the book.

1. _____ Once you've written in your planner, you should not make any changes.

2. _____ Using a top-down strategy means writing down all non-essential items first.

3. _____ If you have a very good memory, it's probably not necessary for you to use a planner.

4. _____ Two items you should gather for writing down important dates are your class syllabi (plural of *syllabus*) and your work schedule.

5. _____ You can use quizzes and worksheets from your class to study for tests.

6. _____ You should be familiar with the process of saving electronic copies of assignments to folders and sub-folders on your computer.

7. _____ It is okay to have music or noise in your workspace if it helps you to concentrate.

8. _____ It's best not to have access to social media sites like Facebook or Twitter while working in your workspace.

9. _____ If clutter doesn't distract you while you're working, then it's not necessary to keep your workspace clutter-free.

10. _____ If you use a room in the library as your workspace, it's important to plan ahead and bring all your supplies and books with you.

Key Terms

Define the following Key Terms from this lesson.

Active Learning:

Digital Planner:

Global Learning:

Learning Style:

Planner:

Reflective Learning:

Syllabus:

Workspace:

Lesson 1.5
Managing Your Time Effectively

OBJECTIVES

★ Create a time budget to manage time more effectively.
★ Learn basic time-management strategies.

BIG IDEA

Creating a time budget can help you manage your time effectively, thereby reducing your stress levels and boosting your productivity.

This lesson will discuss three strategies for managing your time more effectively:

- Use a Time Budget
- Take Breaks
- Avoid Multitasking

Use a Time Budget

Just like a _____ budget shows you how you spend your money, a **time budget** shows you how you spend your _____. You can then _____ "wasted" time that could be used more _____.

Use the following exercises to build your own time budget.

To begin budgeting your time, you first need to get an idea of how you usually spend it. You can do this by creating a record of activities that breaks down your time into increments of 15 minutes.

Here's an example of what your record of activities might look like:

Record of Activities	
Time Block	**Activity**
12:00am – 7:30am	Sleeping
7:30am – 8:15am	Getting ready for class
8:15am – 8:45am	Driving
8:45am – 9:00am	Walking to class
9:00am – 10:30am	Speech class
10:30am – 10:45am	Getting to next class
10:45am – 11:30am	English class

You can use the following template to create your own record of activities.

If you can't track your activities over a full-week span, try to record at least 3-5 days' worth. The goal is to ensure that your record represents how you spend your time in a typical week.

Record of Activities	
Time Block	Activity

Lesson 1.5 | Managing Your Time Effectively

Review the activities you entered and assign each of them to one of the following categories:

- **Sleep** – Time spent sleeping
- **Meal** – Time spent preparing food and eating meals
- **Work** – Time spent at work and any travel time to work
- **Class** – Time spent in class and any travel time to class
- **Study** – Time spent studying and working on class assignments
- **Extracurricular** – Time spent on activities like club meetings, volunteer work, and sports practice
- **Exercise** – Time spent exercising
- **Personal** – Time spent on personal care, laundry, appointments, etc.
- **Family** – Time spent on family commitments
- **Entertainment** – Time spent on hobbies, TV, movies, and the internet
- **Social** – Time spent at parties or with friends
- **Other/Add your own** – Time that doesn't fit into another category

Now, use the table below to add up how many hours you spent on each category. These calculations will help you determine what changes you need to make to budget your time more effectively.

Time Budget Calculator		
Hours	Minutes	Category

Hours	Minutes	Category
Total:	Total:	

Look back at your days of activities and think through the following questions:

1. Do you feel like you had enough time to fulfill all your responsibilities?

2. Were you surprised by how much time was spent on any particular activity?

3. What are some important activities you should have spent more time doing?

4. What are some activities you'd like to spend more time doing in the future?

5. What are some activities you'd like to spend less time doing in the future?

Based on your answers to the previous questions, create a new weekly time budget. Use the following template to prepare your weekly time budget before filling out the next week in your planner.

Lesson 1.5 | Managing Your Time Effectively

Week of: _____

	SUN	MON	TUES	WED	THURS	FRI	SAT
7AM							
8AM							
9AM							
10AM							
11AM							
12PM							
1PM							
2PM							
3PM							
4PM							
5PM							
6PM							
7PM							
8PM							
9PM							
10PM							
11PM							

© HAWKES LEARNING

Take Breaks

After reading about the importance of taking breaks in the lesson, write down in your own words why scheduling breaks is important. What can be the result of studying as long as possible without a break?

Avoid Multitasking

Define the term **multitasking**.

Is multitasking a time-saver? Why or why not?

Lesson Wrap-up

Test Yourself

Next to each statement, write **T** for True or **F** for False. Check your work using the Answer Key in the back of the book.

_____ 1. A time budget is similar to a financial budget.

_____ 2. When planning your time budget, wait until the end of the week and write down everything you did that week.

_____ 3. After you've recorded all the events in one week, you should categorize each activity.

_____ 4. Not taking breaks and overworking your brain is very important if you want to make it through the semester.

_____ 5. Some students perform better if they can look at Facebook and watch TV while they're studying for their next exam.

Write the correct answers in the spaces below. Check your work using the Answer Key in the back of the book.

6. In one week (Monday – Friday) Fred spent 4 hours studying, 10 hours with friends at the student center, and 5 hours watching TV. Which activity did he spend too much time doing?

7. Write down the amount of time Fred should devote to studying (Monday – Sunday) if he has a 3 credit hour class he's supposed to be studying for.

8. If Miguel is taking 12 credit hours this semester, how many hours per week should he devote to studying?

9. What is the name of the strategy which involves writing down the most important activities first in your time budget?

10. How many hours of studying should you set aside for every one hour of class you have?

11. Jane has 10 hours of class each week. She devotes 5 hours of study during the week and weekend. This includes writing papers and studying for tests. Has Jane set aside enough study time?

12. Working on several tasks at the same time is called:

Key Terms

Define the following Key Terms from this lesson.

Multitasking:

Planner:

Study Breaks:

Time Budget:

Lesson 1.6
Taking Notes and Annotating Texts

OBJECTIVE

★ Learn basic listening and note-taking strategies.

BIG IDEA

Good listening and note-taking skills are essential for getting the most out of your class and study times.

In this lesson, you will learn about the following:

- Building Skills in Active Listening
- Effective Note-Taking Methods
- Annotating Texts for Active Reading

Listening Skills

Active listening involves actively paying attention to the _____, asking questions about confusing _____, and making connections to your _____ _____.

Note-Taking

When you are listening in class, _____ down important information will help you pay attention to the _____ and understand the material more _____.

Regardless of the type of notes you take, you should follow a few important guidelines:

- Use _____ _____.
- Use _____ and _____.
- Use your own _____.

Outlines

Outlining class _____ helps you understand the way a topic is _____ by grouping all the information into _____ and _____.

In an **outline**, subtopics are _____ under main topics.

Cornell Notes

Another method for taking notes is the _____ **Method**, a strategy first created by Dr. _____ _____ at Cornell University.

Lesson 1.6 | Taking Notes and Annotating Texts

To take Cornell Notes, divide your paper into _____ sections:

Section 1:

Section 2:

Section 3:

Section 4:

Graphic Organizers

A **graphic organizer** is a note-taking _____ for visually demonstrating relationships _____ ideas.

Mind maps organize the main points of a topic _____.

In the blank mind map below, use the subject of getting a puppy to create your own mind map. Be sure to think of some important topics to consider when raising a dog. Each important topic should have at least one sub-topic.

[Mind map with central oval labeled "Getting a new puppy" connected to six blank boxes]

Annotating

Annotating involves _____ a text and _____ _____ in the margin.

Annotating is a specific type of _____-_____ used for reading assignments outside of _____.

What is the first step before annotating a reading assignment?

Once you've finished, _____ the material again, this time adding _____ and marking important information.

Provide a brief description for each piece of important information:

Definitions:

Important ideas:

Prior knowledge:

Questions:

Summaries:

Answers:

Connections:

Structure:

Lesson Wrap-up

Test Yourself

Next to each statement, write **T** for True or **F** for False. Check your work by using the Answer Key in the back of the book.

1. _____ Good active listening skills are only important for school.
2. _____ A key step in active listening is preparation.
3. _____ One way of avoiding distractions during class is to put your cell phone away.
4. _____ When taking notes, it's important to write down every single word your instructor says.
5. _____ Outlining is the process of dividing your study material into four sections.
6. _____ Annotating is a form of note-taking.

Lesson 1.6 | Taking Notes and Annotating Texts

7. _____ When actively listening in class, it's acceptable to check social media as long as it doesn't interfere with your ability to understand what is going on in class.

8. _____ Taking notes while the instructor is teaching can be part of active listening.

Write the correct answers in the spaces below. Check your work by using the Answer Key in the back of the book.

9. How many times should you read through an assignment before beginning to annotate?

10. Prior knowledge means:

Key Terms

Define the following Key Terms from this lesson.

Active Listening:

Annotating:

Cornell Notes:

Mind Map:

Note Taking:

Outlining:

Prior Knowledge:

Lesson 1.7
Using Effective Study Strategies

OBJECTIVES

★ Learn basic study strategies.
★ Understand the dangers of procrastination.

BIG IDEA

Practicing good study habits now will help you develop the skills you need to excel in later courses.

This lesson will teach you three ways to improve your study habits:

- Make Studying Part of Your Routine
- Use Creative Study Strategies
- Avoid Procrastination

Make Studying Part of Your Routine

Daily studying will keep your mind _____ and ready to receive _____ _____.

To make studying part of your daily routine, try using the following strategies:

- Find _____.

- Schedule _____.

- Be flexible _____.

- Keep _____.

Use Creative Study Strategies

While reviewing class materials is _____, it's not _____.

Everyone has different **learning styles** and _____ preferences. Using a variety of creative _____ _____ will help you find the ones that work best for you. To make the most of your study time, try some of the following _____:

Checklist: Utilizing Creative Study Strategies

✓ Meet _____.

✓ Read _____.

✓ Use _____.

Lesson 1.7 | Using Effective Study Strategies

- ✓ Quiz _____.
- ✓ Use _____.
- ✓ Create _____.
- ✓ Make up _____.

Avoid Procrastination

Define the term **procrastination**.

Procrastination is a _____ idea. Not only will you feel _____ by the amount of information you need to learn, but you may also find yourself with _____ _____ than you can handle.

List some of the factors mentioned in the lesson that cause procrastination and how you might combat them:

- _____
- _____
- _____
- _____
- _____

Lesson Wrap-up

Test Yourself

Next to each statement, write **T** for True and **F** for False. Check your work using the Answer Key in the back of the book.

1. _____ Studying for a test at the last minute is a good idea because that way you have less time to forget all the information.

2. _____ You should study at a time of day when you're most likely to be alert.

3. _____ Once you've established your study time you should never change it.

4. _____ Don't bother studying your notes whenever you have multiple projects due.

5. _____ It's helpful to meet with your instructor and ask how to be successful in the course.

6. _____ Reading your study notes out loud is a waste of time.

7. _____ You should highlight all the text you are studying with just one color.

8. _____ An acronym is an abbreviation using the first letter of each important term.

9. _____ If you procrastinate, you may find that you have more work than you can handle.

10. _____ One cause of procrastination is feeling overwhelmed by a project.

11. _____ Fear or lack of self-confidence is not a major factor in causing procrastination.

12. _____ Good time management can help you avoid the trap of procrastination.

Key Terms

Define the following Key Terms from this lesson.

Acronym:

Learning Style:

Planner:

Procrastination:

Lesson 1.8
Reducing Test Anxiety

OBJECTIVE

★ Explore different strategies for reducing test anxiety.

BIG IDEA

Test anxiety can cause you to become overwhelmed by fear or stress, especially during an assessment. Learning to overcome this anxiety will improve your self-confidence as well as your test performance.

This lesson will discuss three strategies for reducing test anxiety:

- Keep a Positive Attitude
- Know What to Expect
- Use Test-Taking Strategies

Keep a Positive Attitude

How does thinking negatively about yourself and your abilities affect your test-taking skills?

To start thinking more _____, try these strategies:

- Be more _____.
- Praise _____.
- Think _____.
- Find _____.

Know What to Expect

One of the most nerve-wracking aspects of taking a test is the _____. If you've never taken a class with a particular instructor, you may feel _____ about the types of _____ to expect or which _____ to study.

Pre-Test Checklist

- ✓ Meet _____.
- ✓ Take _____.
- ✓ Review _____.
- ✓ Study _____.

Use Test-Taking Strategies

Test-Taking Checklist

✓ _____

✓ _____

✓ _____

✓ _____

✓ _____

Lesson Wrap-up

Test Yourself

Next to each statement, write **T** for True or **F** for False. Check your work using the Answer Key in the back of the book.

1. _____ Tests are a complete picture of every single one of your abilities.

2. _____ You might encounter tests when applying for certain jobs.

3. _____ Speaking and thinking negatively about yourself could affect your test-taking skills because you will lack confidence.

4. _____ Self-confidence plays a large role in how well you perform on tests.

5. _____ Focusing on when you have achieved your goals does not help when preparing for tests.

6. _____ You should think of setbacks as opportunities for growth.

7. _____ Scrolling through Instagram is a great test-prepping ritual.

8. _____ If possible, you should meet with your instructor if you're nervous about a test.

9. _____ A good strategy for preparing for a test would be to look at old quizzes and tests.

10. _____ Your instructor would never let you study in the testing room or classroom.

Key Terms

Define the following Key Terms from this lesson.

Acronym:

Test Anxiety:

Lesson 1.9
Taking Advantage of Campus Resources

OBJECTIVE

★ Identify useful campus resources and services.

BIG IDEA

To get the most value out of your education and boost your academic success, take advantage of all the campus resources offered to you.

In this lesson, you will learn the purpose and services of five common campus organizations:

- Student Services
- The Library
- The Academic Success Center
- The Writing Center
- Disabilities Services

Student Services

Student services is the office responsible for _____ _____.

What are some questions you might want to discuss with your advisor?

1.

2.

3.

4.

The Library

Name a few of the services the library has to offer:

1.

2.

3.

4.

5.

Define the term **LibGuide.**

The Academic Success Center

The **Academic Success Center** exists to help you _____ _____.

Name two ways in which the Academic Success Center can help you:

1.
2.

The Writing Center

The Writing Center offers _____ _____ for all stages of the _____ _____.

To get the most out of your time in the Writing Center, follow these suggestions:

Checklist: Writing Center Visit

✓ _____

✓ _____

✓ _____

✓ _____

Disabilities Services

Disabilities Services assists students who have _____ _____ or _____ _____. One of their main purposes is arranging classroom _____ for students who require assistance in class.

These accommodations might include:

- _____
- _____
- _____

Lesson Wrap-up

Test Yourself

Name the office or resource on campus you would use for each scenario. Check your work using the Answer Key in the back of the book.

1. You need to meet with your advisor:

2. Help in finding particular books or resources:

3. If you feel you needed accommodations such as extra time on tests or projects:

4. If you wanted to discuss career resources:

5. Help in writing a thesis statement for your research paper:

6. If you wanted to schedule an appointment with a tutor:

7. If you wanted to laminate a class project:

8. You need help with a short story for a Creative Writing class:

9. Borrowing a video camera:

10. You need to take tests in a quiet environment:

Key Terms

Define the following Key Terms from this lesson.

Academic Success Center:

Accommodations:

Disabilities Services:

LibGuide:

Library:

Paragraph:

Planner:

Student Services:

Writing Center:

Chapter 2
Reading Skills

Lesson 2.1
Preparing Yourself to Read

OBJECTIVE
- ★ Learn basic pre-reading strategies.

BIG IDEA

Pre-reading activities prepare your mind to get the most out of the time you spend studying and reading.

In this lesson, you will learn three important strategies for pre-reading:
- Scan the Title, Table of Contents, and Major Headings
- Make Predictions and Find Connections
- Create a Plan to Start Reading

Scan the Titles, Table of Contents, and Major Headings

Title

Before you begin a reading, look for a _____ about its contents from the title.

On Your Own

Read the following titles. What would you expect to read about in each of the texts?

"Shortcut to Victory: Inside the Iowa Primary"
Nickel and Dimed
"Opposition to the Vietnam War and the Effect of the Arts"
"College Athletics: Perspectives on the Winners and the Losers"
The Bluest Eye

Table of Contents

The **table of contents** shows you how the information in a book or long document is _____. It might also include a _____ _____ of the topics inside each chapter or section.

© HAWKES LEARNING

Headings and Topic Sentences

Bold _____ and _____ will give you clues about what each section in the reading covers.

Topic sentences usually appear at the _____ of a **paragraph**, and if they are well-written, they should give you a strong idea of what the paragraph will _____.

On Your Own

Consider the following topic sentences. What would you expect to read in the paragraph that each sentence introduces?

Social media is a great way to keep in touch with family and friends.

The researchers soon realized that their original study had major issues.

Despite this opposition, I would argue that the benefits of this business model will outweigh the costs.

Make Predictions and Find Connections

Making predictions will prepare you to think more _____ about a reading.

List the six questions you can ask yourself when making predictions:

1.   4.
2.   5.
3.   6.

READING APPLICATION

Before reading *Taking Care of Beth*, preview its contents and consider how you can make predictions and connections to better understand its meaning. Then, answer the following questions.

What does the title suggest about the story?

Based on the beginning of the story, what can you already tell about the main characters?

What does this tell you about Irving's past?

What is the author trying to tell you about the relationship between Beth and Irving?

What does the author want you to gain from this story?

Create a Plan to Start Reading

Define the term **prior knowledge**.

A **KWL chart** is a useful tool in making _____ between your prior knowledge and your study material.

What do the letters stand for?

K _____

W _____

L _____

READING APPLICATION

Before reading *Ghost in the Machine: Debunking the Paranormal*, apply pre-reading strategies to interact with the text. Utilize the blank KWL chart provided below to guide your pre-reading process, and return to it after reading to note what you learned.

Ghost in the Machine: Debunking the Paranormal

What I Know	What I Want to Know	What I Learned

Reading Plan

List the three questions you can ask yourself as you develop your reading plan:

1.

2.

3.

Lesson Wrap-up

READING APPLICATION

Read the passage *Considerations for Future Dog Owners* and use the annotations as a pre-reading guide.

What is the main idea of each paragraph?

Paragraph 1:

Paragraph 2:

Paragraph 3:

Paragraph 4:

Paragraph 5:

Paragraph 6:

Key Terms

Define the following Key Terms from this lesson.

Abstract:

Active Learning:

Global Learning:

Keywords:

KWL Chart:

Paragraph:

Pre-reading:

Prior Knowledge:

Scholarly Article:

Table of Contents:

Topic Sentence:

Lesson 2.2
Using Visual Clues

OBJECTIVES

★ Recognize different types of charts and graphs.
★ Understand how visual clues add to the meaning of a text.

BIG IDEA

Visual clues such as charts, graphs, pictures, icons, colors, and shapes can add just as much meaning to a text as the actual words do. You need to read these visuals carefully so that you don't miss valuable information.

This lesson will help you identify and understand three types of visual clues:

- Font Design
- Images
- Charts and Graphs

Font Design

Define the term **font**.

When you are pre-reading a text, there are several ways that paying attention to the **font** and **bold headings** can help:

Reading through the titles and headings will help you get a better _____

of your _____.

This information will help you see the overall _____ and

_____ of a reading.

On Your Own

You've been invited to a formal wedding. Which font do you think will appear on the invitation?

    You're Invited   *You're Invited*   You're Invited

READING APPLICATION

Review Tabitha Hawkins' résumé, paying attention to the use of font, italics, spacing, and lines. Below, take notes on how these decisions impact the overall effectiveness of the résumé.

Font:

Italics:

Spacing:

Lines:

Images

What is the first step of analyzing an image?

Define the term **prior knowledge**.

What four questions should you ask yourself when reflecting on your prior knowledge?

1.
2.
3.
4.

Charts and Graphs

Charts and graphs are used to put _____ amounts of _____ into a visual format.

Structure

Bar Graphs

Bar graphs are used to _____ and _____ groups of information.

Pie Charts

Pie charts show _____ of a whole.

Line graphs

Line graphs show _____ over _____.

On Your Own

Which visuals would fit the following sets of data best? Complete the chart below.

Data	Visual
A comparison of sales revenue by restaurant location	
The growing number of Pinterest users since 2010	
The heights of your family members	
A comparison of average grocery costs over the last twelve months	
The average cost of rent in three different cities	

Data

The _____ will give you a clear idea of the data being illustrated in the chart or graph.

You can then read the **legend**, which shows you the _____ or _____ that represent each group of information.

Finally, read the _____ and _____ on each part of the chart or graph. This will show you how the data is _____ together.

Lesson Wrap-up

READING APPLICATION

Read the passage about minimum wage and answer the following questions.

What is the overall topic of this passage?

What terms might you need to define during your pre-reading activities?

What kind of visual is used in the passage?

Key Terms

Define the following Key Terms from this lesson.

Bar Graph:

Data:

Font:

Legend:

Line Graph:

Pie Chart:

Visual Clue:

Lesson 2.3
Reading Actively and Purposefully

OBJECTIVES

- ★ Identify helpful strategies to check understanding.
- ★ Identify review strategies.
- ★ Learn a process for active reading.
- ★ Understand the differences between active and passive reading.

BIG IDEA

Active reading is a process that focuses your attention on what you are reading so that you can and retain the material.

Define the term **passive reading**.

This lesson will teach you how to use active reading strategies to get the most from your reading.

- Make Pre-reading a Priority
- Check Your Understanding
- Review What You Learned

Make Pre-reading a Priority

What steps should you follow during pre-reading?

1.

2.

3.

4.

READING APPLICATION

Read the passage *Rules for Celebrity Ads on Social Media*. As you read, answer the annotation questions below.

How can you connect to this idea? Where have you seen celebrities in advertising lately?

Now that you've finished reading, consider how this information built upon what you already knew.

© HAWKES LEARNING

Check Your Understanding

If you are having a difficult time staying on task, try _____ _____ _____ to yourself.

Summarize Paragraphs

Define the term **summary**.

Summarizing each paragraph will help you identify areas where you did not _____ the reading.

READING APPLICATION

Practice checking your understanding as you read the passage about attraction.

Review What You Learned

What are the four steps of the final stage of the active reading process?

1.
2.
3.
4.

Lesson Wrap-up

READING APPLICATION

Read the passage *Battle of the Parties: Supreme Court Edition*. As you read the passage, consider how you can apply active reading strategies to comprehend the author's meaning.

What is the topic of the passage?

Summarize the author's message.

Test Yourself

Next to each question, write **Y** for Yes or **N** for No. Check your work using the Answer Key in the back of the book.

1. _____ Sarah is reading the chapter as quickly as possible and looks at Facebook every five minutes to see if anyone commented on her photo. Is she practicing active reading?

2. _____ Jose is doing a KWL chart and looking up unfamiliar words. He also looked at all the bold headings in his reading material. Is he practicing active reading?

3. _____ Jane has been assigned a chapter on communism. She remembers something she learned about the Cold War that is related to this subject. She is looking up that information and thinking about what she knows. Is she activating her prior knowledge?

Key Terms

Define the following Key Terms from this lesson.

Active Reading:

Conclusion:

Introduction:

Passive Reading:

Reading Comprehension:

Summary:

Lesson 2.4
Deconstructing Topics, Ideas, and Details

OBJECTIVES

- ★ Distinguish between general and specific information.
- ★ Distinguish between major and minor details.
- ★ Distinguish between topic and support sentences.
- ★ Recognize general topics and main ideas.

BIG IDEA

Identifying the main idea, topics, and details will help you analyze texts more effectively.

In this lesson, you will learn how to deconstruct the components of a text using these strategies:

- Distinguish Between General and Specific Information
- Recognize the General Topic
- Locate the Main Idea
- Break Down the Supporting Details
- Annotate the Paragraph

Distinguish Between General and Specific Information

Explain the difference between **general information** and **specific information**.

Examples:

General Information	dog
Specific Information	German Shepherd
	Basset Hound
	Corgi

On Your Own

Use the table to fill in your own examples of general and specific information. The first row has been completed for you.

General	Specific
States	Florida, Tennessee, South Carolina

Lesson 2.4 | Deconstructing Topics, Ideas, and Details

READING APPLICATION

Read the passage *How to Keep Texting Language from Affecting Our Communication.*

Write in your own words what general information is covered in the first paragraph of the passage.

What specific information from the passage provides ideas for how to deal with the situation raised in the first paragraph? (Hint: Look for this information in paragraphs 2 and 4.)

In your own words below, write a brief summary of the passage's general information and the specific solutions to improve the issue.

General and Specific Components of a Text

Define each of the following components, or parts, of a text:

Topic:

Main Idea:

Supporting Details:

Recognize the General Topic

What two questions can you use to identify the topic of a text?

1.
2.

Locate the Main Idea

Define the term **main idea**.

List the questions you should consider to determine the main idea of a text:

1.
2.
3.

© HAWKES LEARNING

Break Down the Supporting Details   47

READING APPLICATION

Read the passage *Building a Safer School Environment* and consider how the author expresses the topic and main idea in the first paragraph. Then, complete the chart below.

Topic	Purpose	Main Idea

Topic Sentence

A well-written topic sentence must meet several requirements:

- _____
- _____
- _____

Break Down the Supporting Details

Define the term **major details**.

Define the term **minor details**.

Annotate the Paragraph

Read the annotated paragraph about Kettering and notice how specific information is highlighted and underlined. Then, answer the following questions.

What is the topic of this paragraph?

What are the details listed in the body of the paragraph that support the topic?

The last two paragraphs list the factors that contributed to the changes in the neighborhood. What are they?

© HAWKES LEARNING

Lesson Wrap-up

READING APPLICATION

Read the passage *Pause Before You Post: Social Media Etiquette* and answer the following questions.

What is the topic?

What is the author's purpose?

In the second paragraph, what transition phrase signals the underlined minor detail?

Identify one major detail in paragraph 4.

At the end of the passage, how does the author restate the topic sentence?

What is the author's conclusion?

Key Terms

Write the number of each term next to its definition; then, check your answers with the Key Terms list at the end of Lesson 2.4.

1. Topic
2. Main Idea
3. General Information
4. Specific Information
5. Signal/Signpost Word

_____ A word or word group that can be linked to a broad range of specific ideas and details

_____ The general subject of a text

_____ A word or word group that introduces a new idea and/or shows the connection between two ideas

_____ The statement or argument that an author tries to communicate

_____ A word or idea with a narrow focus

Define the following Key Terms from this lesson.

Annotation:

Major Detail:

Minor Detail:

Paragraph:

Purpose:

Supporting Detail:

Topic Sentence:

Lesson 2.5
Identifying Organizational Patterns

OBJECTIVE
★ Identify different types of organizational patterns.

BIG IDEA

Knowing the organizational pattern of a paragraph or other written text can help you understand the author's train of thought.

Define the term **organizational pattern**.

This lesson will describe six types of organizational patterns:

- Cause and Effect
- Chronological
- Compare and Contrast
- Order of Importance
- Spatial
- Topical

Cause and Effect

Writing that is organized by **cause and effect** explains the _____ or _____ of a topic.

Complete the following chart by listing the corresponding effect of each cause. For example, if it is snowing (cause), the roads will be slippery (effect).

Cause	Effect
The baby is hungry.	
It has rained for five days.	

Complete the following chart by listing the corresponding cause of each effect. For example, if a person's car has a flat tire (effect), it may be due to a nail in the tire (cause).

Cause	Effect
	No one wants to eat at that restaurant.
	People are cheering outside of a church as a couple walks out.

Lesson 2.5 | Identifying Organizational Patterns

A book or document organized by cause and effect will use **signal words** that show _____ or _____.

Write three signal words or phrases that show *why* or *how*:

1.
2.
3.

READING APPLICATION

Read the passage about revolutionary France and think about how the organization and word choice indicate cause and effect. Then, answer the questions below.

What is the cause given in the first paragraph?

Provide one positive and one negative effect found in the passage.

Positive Effect: **Negative Effect:**

Chronological

When a text is arranged _____, the author discusses the ideas or events in the order that they _____.

When you're reading a chronological text, look for signal words that indicate _____.

List three signal words or phrases that indicate time:

1.
2.
3.

READING APPLICATION

Read the passage about the role of sports in Europe. How does the author indicate the passage of time?

Compare and Contrast

The **compare and contrast** organizational pattern is used to show the _____ and _____ between two topics.

List three compare and contrast signal words or phrases below:

1.

2.

3.

READING APPLICATION

Read the essay about pet ownership. Then, complete the following chart using examples from the passage.

Owning Cats and Dogs: Similarities	Owning Cats and Dogs: Differences

List three compare and contrast signal words or phrases in the passage:

1.

2.

3.

Order of Importance

When a text is organized by **order of importance**, the information is arranged from _____ _____ to _____ _____ or vice versa.

List three signal words or phrases that show importance:

1.

2.

3.

Lesson 2.5 | Identifying Organizational Patterns

READING APPLICATION

Read the essay about classroom size. Then, answer the following questions:

What is the topic of this essay?

What signal phrase is used at the beginning of paragraph 2?

According to paragraph 2, what is an important reason for reducing class size?

Is this essay organized from most important reason to least important or from least important to most important? How do you know?

Spatial

Spatial organization is used to describe a topic by its _____ _____.

A spatial text will use words that show _____.

Write three spatial signal words or phrases:

1.
2.
3.

Use spatial signal words to describe your location in two or three sentences.

READING APPLICATION

As you read the passage about Ron visiting his childhood home, look for indicators of space, location, and direction. List two examples that you find:

1.
2.

Topical

Topical organization is a general organizational pattern used for _____ _____ main points.

List three signal words used in topically organized texts:

1.

2.

3.

READING APPLICATION

Read the passage about mosquito repellants and identify its topic and main idea:

Lesson Wrap-up

Test Yourself

Write the number of each organizational pattern next to the corresponding topic sentence. Check your work using the Answer Key in the back of the book.

1. Cause and Effect
2. Chronological
3. Compare and Contrast
4. Order of Importance
5. Spatial

a. _____ There are several major differences between buying a home and renting one.

b. _____ As I stepped into the boys' room, I could see evidence of the big party they had.

c. _____ This recent hurricane had many devastating effects on south Florida.

d. _____ The American Civil War began in 1861 and ended in 1865.

e. _____ There are many important issues to consider when selecting a pet for your family.

Key Terms

Define the following Key Terms from this lesson.

Organizational Pattern:

Paragraph:

Signal/Signpost Word:

Topical:

Lesson 2.6
Using Context for Unfamiliar Words or Phrases

OBJECTIVE
★ Recognize the different types of context clues.

BIG IDEA

Context clues will help you discover the meaning of unfamiliar words by piecing together the meanings with clues found in the text. You don't always have access to Google or the dictionary, so learning to use context clues will help you better understand the reading material.

Define the term **context clue**.

In this lesson, you will learn how to find the meaning of a word based on context clues:
- Look for Clues in Nearby Sentences
- Use Substitution to Test Possible Meanings

Look for Clues in Nearby Sentences

What is the first step of finding the meaning of an unfamiliar word?

Definition

Example:

Imagine my humiliation when my friends tricked me into wearing a silly costume to the fancy dinner party. I've never been that embarrassed before.

Based on the context clue, what is the meaning of *humiliation*?

Synonym

A **synonym** is a word that has the _____ meaning as another word. Authors sometimes use a _____ and a _____ to add extra emphasis or explanation to the sentence.

Example:

The spoiled meat was so putrid, or smelly, that I had to plug my nose.

In this sentence, the meaning of the word *putrid* is the same as the word *smelly*. The author included both words to make sure the audience understands the meaning.

In the following sentence, choose the synonym context clue for the word *obedient*.

> Even though my dog, Pippa, lacks formal training, she is quite obedient, or well-behaved, by nature.

Antonym

An **antonym** is a word that has the _____ meaning of another word.

List three signal words that indicate the use of an antonym:

1.
2.
3.

In the following sentence, choose the antonym context clue for the word *scorching*.

> I expected the temperatures here to be scorching, but they're actually quite cool.

> Based on the context clue, what is the meaning of *scorching*?

Example

Authors sometimes use _____ to explain the meaning of a difficult word. These examples often follow the phrase *for example*.

In the following sentence, indicate the example that explains the meaning of *detests*.

> Sarah detests most kinds of seafood; for example, she can't stand the taste of lobster.

Inference

An **inference** is a _____ _____ based on what's happening in the text.

Read the following example and use inference to explain the meaning of *gridlock*.

> Every morning during rush hour, the gridlock on the freeway is so bad that it takes me an hour to get to work.

Use Substitution to Test Possible Meanings

To use substitution, think of a possible _____ and read the sentence with that word.

Example:

Each time it snows, I feel the overwhelming need to hibernate; it takes me forever to get anything done.

Use substitution to explain the meaning of *hibernate*.

On Your Own

Read the following paragraph and use context clues to determine the meanings of the underlined words in the space below.

> Nutritional science is effectively a 20th century creation. On the basics of what the human animal ought to eat, as expressed in dietary recommendations around the world, the experts more or less agree (Cannon). However, on many specific issues there are differences of view that are intense and even polemical in character. Obesity is one area of conspicuous contention. In part, these disputes reflect the youth of the science. They also reflect the practical difficulties of conducting long-term, controlled research on the daily routines of numerous human subjects. The consequence is that many non-nutritionists working on obesity have difficulty finding agreed, actionable conclusions from nutritional science on what to do about the problem.

Dietary:

Polemical:

Contention:

Actionable:

Lesson Wrap-up

Test Yourself

Answer the following questions. Check your work using the Answer Key in the back of the book.

1. What is an antonym for *happy*?

2. What kind of context clue is being used in the following sentence?

    The once feral cat became tame once she got to know us.

3. What is a synonym for *frightened*?

4. What kind of context clue is being used in the following sentence?

The elderly man was not stable after his surgery. He fell down multiple times.

5. What is the signal word indicating the use of an antonym in the following sentence?

The moon was radiant tonight, unlike last night when it was hidden behind the clouds.

Key Terms

Define the following Key Terms from this lesson.

Antonym:

Context Clue:

Example:

Inference:

Paragraph:

Synonym:

Lesson 2.7
Using Word Parts for Unfamiliar Words

OBJECTIVE

★ Identify the meaning of a word from word parts.

BIG IDEA

Like context clues, word parts can help you figure out meanings of unfamiliar words.

This lesson will teach you how to use word parts to find the meanings of words.

Roots

The _____ is the main part of a word and contains the basic _____ of the word. _____ _____ are roots that can stand alone without any other word parts.

_____ _____ are another type of root. They form the _____ of a word but cannot stand _____ their _____. They must always be _____ with other word parts.

Describe what you think each of the following words means based on the shared root, *auto*.

Autobiography:

Automatically:

Autonomy:

Define the term **word family**.

Prefixes

Prefixes are a second type of word part that are added to the _____ of roots to create new words.

To complete the following table from the lesson, add the meaning of each common prefix.

Prefix	Meaning
bi-	
co-	
de-	

mis-	
non-, un-	
post-	
pre-	
re-	
semi-	
trans-	
uni-	

Suffixes

Suffixes are added _____ a _____ to change the meaning of a word.

To complete the following table from the lesson, add the meaning of each common suffix.

Suffix	Meaning
-able	
-ance, -ence	
-ful	
-fy	
-ion, -sion, -tion	
-ize	
-less	
-ly	
-ness	
-ology	
-or, -er	

Lesson 2.7 | Using Word Parts for Unfamiliar Words

On Your Own

Look at the following words and use the roots, prefixes, and suffixes from this lesson to determine their meanings and complete the following chart.

Word	Meaning
Judicator	
Graphology	
Autophobia	
Diction	

Lesson Wrap-up

Key Terms

Define the following Key Terms from this lesson.

Combining Root:

Context Clue:

Prefix:

Root:

Root Word:

Suffix:

Word Family:

Lesson 2.8
Making Inferences About a Text

OBJECTIVE
- ★ Learn strategies for making inferences about a text.

BIG IDEA

Authors do not always directly state everything they want their readers to know about a topic. It's sometimes up to the reader to make a logical conclusion in order to gain full understanding of the text.

Define the term **inference**.

List the three factors that inferences are based on:

1.

2.

3.

What are some questions you can answer by making inferences?

1.

2.

3.

4.

5.

The ability to make educated guesses based on clues in the text is essential for

_____ _____.

In this lesson, you will learn how to make inferences about a text using three steps:
- Activate Your Prior Knowledge
- Look for Clues
- Ask Yourself Questions

Activate Your Prior Knowledge

Define the term **prior knowledge**.

Drawing inferences is all about finding _____ in _____ and _____.

Look for Clues

Define the term **implied information**.

Visuals

The _____ inside a text can help you understand the author's _____ and _____. You need to think about _____ the author decided to include a particular photo or illustration. Visuals can also help you make connections to your _____ _____.

Tone

Define the term **tone**.

Organization

The **organizational pattern** of a text can contain clues about the author's _____ and _____ _____. As you read, look for _____ _____ that might indicate the type of organization.

READING APPLICATION

Read the article *First Impressions* and notice how you can infer information about the author's message because of the deliberate tone and organization.

What is the author's purpose of this article as stated in the last sentence of the first paragraph?

Would you say the overall tone of this passage is positive or negative? Explain your answer.

Ask Yourself Questions

Write the questions that you should ask yourself as a final step in making logical inferences based on the textual clues you've found:

1.
2.
3.
4.
5.
6.

Lesson Wrap-up

READING APPLICATION

Read the narrative excerpt *Uncle Ted* and see what you can infer based upon the author's suggestions. Then, answer the following questions.

What information indicates that Uncle Ted is a farmer?

How do you know Uncle Ted likes the person who is telling the story?

Is Uncle Ted a good cook? How do you know?

Key Terms

Define the following Key Terms from this lesson.

Cause and Effect:

Chronological:

Compare and Contrast:

Inference:

KWL Chart:

Main Idea:

Order of Importance:

Organizational Pattern:

Pre-reading:

Prior Knowledge:

Purpose:

Reading Comprehension:

Spatial:

Tone:

Topical:

Verbal Learning:

Lesson 2.9
Recognizing Types of Main Ideas and Evidence

OBJECTIVES

★ Identify different types of supporting details.
★ Recognize the main idea in a text.

BIG IDEA

Identifying main ideas and supporting details in a text can help you understand it more thoroughly. Also, being able to pinpoint the types and locations of supporting evidence allows you to decide whether or not the evidence effectively supports the main idea.

In this lesson, you will learn about the following:

- Recognizing the Main Idea(s)
- Recognizing Types of Evidence
- Analyzing the Supporting Details

Recognizing the Main Idea(s)

A topic is the most _____ characteristic of a _____. The main idea is the more _____ claim the author makes *about* the _____.

When pointing out the main idea, the author answers this question: What do I want my readers to _____ or _____ after reading this text?

For each of the following topics, think of a claim (what you want readers to understand or believe) and complete the table.

Topic	Claim
Price of school lunches	
Homework in college	
Raising taxes on families	

Define the term **paragraph**.

Define the term **topic sentence**.

READING APPLICATION

Read the excerpt from the essay on the evolution of technology.

In your own words, what is the paragraph's main idea?

Implied main ideas are often used when the author is writing to _____ or _____.

Thesis and Purpose Statements

In a _____ text, the main ideas of each _____ serve to make claims that support a bigger idea. This bigger idea is usually indicated in a thesis statement or statement of purpose.

Define the term **thesis statement**.

Define the term **purpose statement**.

Where are purpose statements most commonly found?

Choose an example thesis and purpose statement provided in the text and explain what evidence might support the statement.

Thesis Statement

Example:

Possible supporting evidence:

Purpose Statement

Example:

Possible supporting evidence:

Lesson 2.9 | Recognizing Types of Main Ideas and Evidence

Locating the Thesis

Try following these steps to locate the thesis statement:

1. Find the _____ _____ of each _____.

2. Form the _____ _____ into a _____ paragraph.

3. Determine the _____ _____ of the summary paragraph to find the _____.

Recognizing Types of Evidence

_____ _____ are the specific pieces of information that are used to support a main idea.

Supporting details often answer questions that start with _____, _____, _____, _____, _____, and _____.

There are several types of information that an author can use to support main ideas. Define each term:

Anecdotes:

Descriptions:

Examples:

Expert Analysis:

Facts:

Reflections:

Statistics:

Analyzing the Supporting Details

The _____ and _____ of the text will influence the types of supporting details that the author uses.

List the questions you can use to determine how well supporting details support a main idea:

1.

2.

3.

Read the paragraph and answer the following questions.

> Every year, World Malaria Day forces us to look at where we came from, where we are, and what still needs to be done. Joint action over the past decade has led to an impressive impact: malaria infection rates have been cut in half, and 4.3 million lives have been saved ("World Malaria Report 2014"). Fifty-five countries are on track to reach the World Health Assembly target of a 75% reduction in their malaria burden by 2015 ("World Malaria Report 2014"). Although these huge gains are impressive, they remain fragile if the momentum of the joint action cannot be maintained. Clearly, not keeping the momentum leads to the resurgence of malaria, as we have experienced in numerous previous elimination efforts at national or subnational level.

What is the main idea of the paragraph?

What two statistics does the author use to support the main idea?

1.

2.

Lesson Wrap-up

READING APPLICATION

Read the persuasive essay titled *Arts Programs*. As you read, take note of the author's claims and supporting details. Then, answer the questions below.

What is the thesis statement?

Lesson 2.9 | Recognizing Types of Main Ideas and Evidence

What evidence is used to support the thesis statement? Provide two examples.

1.
2.

Key Terms

Define the following Key Terms from this lesson.

Anecdote:

Description:

Evidence:

Example:

Expert Analysis:

Fact:

Implied Main Idea:

Introduction:

Main Idea:

Paragraph:

Purpose:

Purpose Statement:

Reflection:

Signal/Signpost Word:

Statistic:

Supporting Detail:

Thesis Statement:

Topic Sentence:

Chapter 3
Critical Thinking

Lesson 3.1
Identifying Purpose and Tone

OBJECTIVES

★ Recognize the purpose of a text.
★ Understand how tone adds to the meaning of a text.

BIG IDEA

Authors use purpose and tone as tools to help their readers better understand what they're trying to say. As a reader, you must think critically about the *why* and the *how* behind a text. This will give a more complete understanding of what an author is trying to say.

In this lesson, you will learn how to identify the following:

- Author's Purpose
- Author's Tone

Author's Purpose

List the four most common **purposes** for writing:

1.   3.

2.   4.

To Inform

The author of an **informative** text wants to give the audience _____ about a topic.

Name three texts that commonly seek to inform:

1.

2.

3.

To Persuade

The author of a **persuasive** text wants to _____ the audience to adopt a _____ or take an _____.

Name three texts that commonly seek to persuade:

1.
2.
3.

To Narrate

The author of a **narrative** text wants to _____ and _____ on a personal _____ or _____.

Name three texts that commonly seek to narrate:

1.
2.
3.

To Entertain

The author of an **entertaining** text wants to _____ the reader by _____ a _____ or _____ in a _____ or _____ way.

Name three kinds of texts that commonly seek to entertain:

1.
2.
3.

Tone

Tone is the _____ expressed about the topic of the text. Authors use _____ and _____ carefully to establish a clear tone. Tone is usually described using adjectives that are _____, _____, or _____.

Tone

Complete the table below using adjectives that describe the tone of a text. There are some ideas in the lesson, but try to think of your own as well.

Positive	Negative	Neutral

In most cases, tone is not stated _____; instead, the reader has to _____ _____ _____ _____ to determine how the author feels about the topic.

The first indication of the author's tone is _____ _____.

Look at the chart of **synonyms** in the lesson and think about how you respond differently to each one. Then, look at the examples below and consider how word choice affects the overall tone of the sentence.

My dad bought my mom an affordable diamond ring for their anniversary.

My dad bought my mom a cheap diamond ring for their anniversary.

Complete the following table. For each word, think of a synonym with the opposite tone. Look up any unfamiliar words.

Negative	Positive
	thrifty
	outgoing
reeks	
cowardly	

A text that uses words without any strongly _____ or _____ meanings is trying to be as _____ and _____ as possible.

The second way to identify an author's tone is to consider the details that have been _____ or _____.

List the five questions you can ask yourself to determine an author's tone:

1.
2.
3.
4.
5.

© HAWKES LEARNING

Indicate the positive language in the following sentences.

> After the tornado swept through the town, the community immediately supported everyone who had suffered losses. Friends, neighbors, and strangers united in a way that transformed the entire area.

On Your Own

Read the following online review, paying close attention to the details. What is the overall tone of this review? Check the box next to your answer.

> My husband and I visited Marion Diner on the recommendation of a friend who is also a local food blogger. As we were walking into the restaurant, we were greeted with the delicious scent of sautéed garlic and rosemary. The waiter was friendly and knowledgeable about the menu. She even recommended her personal favorites. The menu itself was not lengthy at all. Clearly, this restaurant focuses on a few key specialties and customer favorites. I was surprised to see the blend of fresh, healthy ingredients incorporated into traditional "diner food."
>
> I ordered the Bleu Ribbon Burger with baked onion straws, and my husband had the Grandstand Salad. My burger was cooked perfectly, although the onion straws were more seasoned than I would have preferred. I'm not a salad fan, but even I had to admit that my husband's meal looked great.
>
> Overall, I would definitely recommend Marion to anyone who's looking for a fresh twist on well-loved diner favorites.

☐ Positive ☐ Negative ☐ Neutral

Lesson Wrap-up

READING APPLICATION

Read the example blog post in the lesson. Pay attention to the annotations in the margins and the author's choice of language.

Read the letter written by a concerned community member. How do the tone and purpose of this writing compare to the previous blog post you just read?

What is the author's purpose for writing the letter?

Test Yourself

Next to each question, write **E** for entertain, **I** for inform, **P** for persuade, or **R** for reflect. Check your work using the Answer Key in the back of the book.

1. _____ What is most likely the purpose of a comic book?
2. _____ What is most likely the purpose of a science textbook?
3. _____ What is most likely the purpose of a children's fiction novel about the life of a unicorn?
4. _____ If an author says that childhood vaccines should be mandatory, what is his or her purpose?
5. _____ If an author writes about childhood experiences in Lebanon, what is his or her purpose?
6. _____ If an author tries to be as objective and unbiased as possible, what is his or her purpose?

Next to each statement, write **T** for True or **F** for False.

7. _____ To understand a text fully, it's important to know the author's purpose.
8. _____ An author would never be dishonest about his or her true purpose for writing.
9. _____ A text with a neutral tone just gives the facts in a straightforward way.
10. _____ A textbook will generally have a neutral tone.

Key Terms

Write the number of each term next to its definition.

1. Tone
2. Persuasive Text
3. Informative Text
4. Entertaining Text
5. Reflective Text

_____ A text that explores a topic or event in a creative or humorous way

_____ A text that gives the audience information about a topic

_____ A text that convinces its audience to adopt a belief or take an action

_____ A text that shares a personal experience or belief

_____ The positive, negative, or neutral attitude that an author expresses about a topic

Define the following Key Terms from this lesson.

Purpose:

Synonym:

Topic:

Visual Learning:

Word Choice:

Lesson 3.2
Analyzing Argumentation Strategies

OBJECTIVE

★ Analyze the argumentation strategies used in a text.

BIG IDEA

When reading a text, it is helpful to recognize the type of argument it makes; this will help you make an informed decision based on your analysis.

Arguments can be broken into three basic parts:
- *Ethos*, an argument based on a person's credibility
- *Logos*, an argument based on logic
- *Pathos*, an argument based on emotion

Ethos, *logos*, and *pathos* can be found in any newspaper, magazine, blog, or tweet. All of these texts are trying to _____ you in some way.

While an advertisement or opinion article is clearly pushing you to buy a specific product or believe a certain thing, other texts use argumentation strategies for _____ other than persuading.

Imagine that you are reading an article about the history of the telephone. The author's main purpose is to _____. Whether or not the author realizes it, however, he or she is also trying to convince you that his or her article is true and reliable.

This lesson will teach you how to analyze the *ethos*, *logos*, and *pathos* in an argument.

Ethos

Ethos is an argument based on _____.

Define the term **credibility**.

An effective text will use the _____ of experts to argue its points.

Think about the types of people you would consider experts. What are their credentials? Fill in the blanks below.

One type of *ethos* is a person's professional _____.

You should also consider personal _____.

Ethos can also be based on a person's _____.

When faced with new _____, make sure to always check the _____ of the information.

Keep in mind that *ethos* does not guarantee that an argument is _____. Plenty of experts within the same field disagree or even contradict each other. A good argument will use a _____ of *ethos*, *logos*, and *pathos* to prove its point.

READING APPLICATION

Read the historical excerpt in the lesson and note how the author uses *ethos* to support her argument. In the first sentence, how does the author establish her credentials in this subject?

What are the two other credible sources cited in this passage?
1.
2.

Logos

Logos is an argument based on _____.

A **logical argument** makes a _____ claim using _____ _____ like _____ and _____.

Facts can be _____ and are accepted by the majority of experts in the field.

Statistics represent _____ from _____ _____, and they are most accurate when gathered from a wide range of research methods and samples.

Example:
> 75% of dentists who took the survey agreed that Toothy Tooth is the best toothpaste for fighting cavities.

Keep in mind that not all facts and statistics are _____. Always be on the lookout for clues that a source might be _____ or _____, as these factors could impact the validity of the information.

Pathos

Pathos is an appeal to _____.

Consider the following sentences:
> Marcia was sad when the family reunion was over.

Marcia was devastated to leave her family after a wonderful week together; she didn't know when she might see them again.

Which sentence is more expressive and powerful? Why do you think so?

Emotions can also be communicated through the _____ or _____ that an author chooses to include in a text. These stories help the audience _____ _____ to the logical information being presented.

A reliable text will use emotion to support its argument, not to _____ its audience.

READING APPLICATION

Read the passage *Unfair Dog Banning Has Permanent Consequences*. Notice the image located under the title. Provide three examples of language that the author uses to appeal to readers' emotions.

1.
2.
3.

Lesson Wrap-up

On Your Own

Read the following descriptions and check the box next to the argumentation strategy being described.

An argument based on a person's credibility.
- ☐ *Logos*
- ☐ *Ethos*
- ☐ *Pathos*

An argument based on emotion.
- ☐ *Logos*
- ☐ *Ethos*
- ☐ *Pathos*

An argument based on logic.
- ☐ *Logos*
- ☐ *Ethos*
- ☐ *Pathos*

Lesson Wrap-up

READING APPLICATION

Read the letter in the lesson that incorporates all three argumentation strategies. Using the annotations as help, consider how the author deliberately appeals to her audience.

Test Yourself

Next to each statement that uses an argumentation strategy, write **E** for *Ethos*, **P** for *Pathos*, or **L** for *Logos*. Check your work using the Answer Key in the back of the book.

1. _____ A recent survey reported a 95% increase in pet owners who have their pets spayed or neutered.
2. _____ The head nurse says the nurses need an updated policies and procedures handbook.
3. _____ What kind of society have we become when so many teenagers are using drugs?
4. _____ Mr. Hammond has been on the board of education for twenty years.
5. _____ Statistically, it is safer to fly than to drive. One in ten drivers will have a car accident.
6. _____ The devastating flood wiped out many homes in our area and traumatized the people.

Key Terms

Write the number of each term next to its definition.

7. *Logos*
8. *Ethos*
9. Credibility
10. Conclusion
11. *Pathos*
12. Persuasive Text

_____ An argument based on a person's credibility

_____ A text that convinces its audience to adopt a belief or take an action

_____ What makes someone or something believable

_____ An argument that makes a reasonable claim, usually using facts and statistics

_____ An argument based on emotion

_____ The result of a logical argument

Define the following Key Terms from this lesson.

Argument:

Evidence:

Example:

Fact:

Logical Argument:

Supporting Detail:

Lesson 3.3
Identifying Bias

OBJECTIVE

★ Identify bias in a text.

BIG IDEA

All authors have life experiences that shape their personal opinions. These opinions usually affect their writing, so it's important to spot bias in a text and decide how it impacts the author's overall argument.

List five factors that influence a person's opinions and preferences:

1.

2.

3.

4.

5.

This lesson will help you evaluate three areas of a text for bias:

- Purpose
- Tone
- Supporting Details

Purpose

The first step in identifying bias is to _____ the author's _____ for writing.

In a biased text, the _____ purpose may not be the same as the _____ purpose.

Define the term **agenda**.

Thinking about purpose will also help you identify a _____ of _____.

Conflicts of interest happen when the author has a _____ _____ in a topic.

As you evaluate the purpose of a text, ask yourself these questions:

1.

2.

3.

4.

5.

Tone

Define the term **tone**.

Selecting extremely negative or positive words often signals that the author is trying to
_____ the _____.

Rewrite the following sentence so that it uses a neutral tone.

> The horrific woman left her helpless dog alone in the car for 15 entire minutes.

Use the following questions to evaluate the tone of a text:

1.

2.

3.

Authors sometimes use _____ to put a topic in a more positive light.

One final way that tone indicates bias is the use of stereotypes or _____ _____ about a person's age, ethnicity, gender, or religion. This is almost always an indication that the piece of writing contains _____ against certain groups of people.

READING APPLICATION

Read the persuasive letter and consider how language creates a strong tone and clear bias toward one side of the argument. Pay attention to the annotations.

In the first sentence, what are the two emotionally charged words the author uses?

1.

2.

What information does the author give about herself in the beginning of the letter that explains why she is biased toward the arts program?

What would you say is the overall tone of the letter?

Supporting Details

The final way to detect bias in a text is to examine the _____ _____, or evidence, that the author chooses to include or exclude.

List some clues that might help you detect bias in a writing:

A biased text will leave out _____ that doesn't _____ its point.

An unbiased author will acknowledge other _____, even if he/she doesn't spend time discussing each one.

Lesson Wrap-up

READING APPLICATION

Read the passage about local policy change. How does the author's use of tone, purpose, and supporting detail suggest bias, even in a short paragraph?

List two examples of emotionally-charged language in the paragraph that indicate the writer's bias:

1.

2.

READING APPLICATION

Read the passage titled *Worried About Your Browsing Privacy? Trust Us!*, written by Cleveland Cable, a national cable provider.

What can you determine about the overall purpose and tone of this piece?

How are supporting details used to further the company's agenda?

What is this company's agenda?

Key Terms

Beside each definition, write the corresponding term.

_____: A person's hidden motive

_____: A reason why you should think or act a certain way

_____: A person's opinions and preferences

_____: When an author has a personal stake in a topic that affects his purpose

_____: A piece of information, also called a supporting detail, that is used to support a main idea

_____: A specific instance or illustration that demonstrates a point

_____: Disrespectful language that refers to a person's gender, ethnicity or culture, physical or mental ability, or sexual orientation

_____: A piece of information that most people generally agree to be true

_____: A text that gives the audience information about a topic

_____: A short piece of writing that focuses on one main idea

_____: A text that convinces its audience to adopt a belief or take an action

_____: The goal of a text

_____: Making a topic seem more positive than it actually is

_____: A piece of information, also called evidence, that is used to support a main idea

_____: The positive, negative, or neutral attitude that an author expresses about a topic

Lesson 3.4
Evaluating Evidence

OBJECTIVE

★ Evaluate the supporting details used in a text.

BIG IDEA

In order to determine whether or not an author's supporting details are trustworthy, it's important to know how to evaluate the evidence in a text.

This lesson will help you evaluate evidence based on three conditions:

- Accuracy
- Credibility
- Relevance

Write the seven commonly used types of supporting details and their definitions:

1.

2.

3.

4.

5.

6.

7.

Accuracy

The first step in examining evidence is checking for _____.

What four questions can you use to examine evidence for accuracy?

1.   3.

2.   4.

Evidence based on research, such as facts and statistics, should be clearly explained by the authors or researchers.

Be cautious of any facts or statistics that use words like _____, _____, or _____.

When you are evaluating evidence based on personal experience, make sure there are _____ details about the _____.

Watch out for evidence that seems overly _____ or _____.

Credibility

To prove that the evidence in a text is _____, the author must demonstrate that the information comes from a **credible** source.

Credible evidence comes from an _____ in the _____.

The _____ and _____ of an expert source should match the evidence.

Non-expert _____ is acceptable as long as the source has _____ experience in the topic.

READING APPLICATION

Read the passage *Do Vaccines Cause Autism?* and consider the credibility. Then, answer the questions below.

What are the credentials of the psychologist as cited by the author?

What is the credible source cited in paragraph 2?

What is the bias mentioned in the annotation near the end of the passage?

What do you think is the author's overall purpose for writing this article?

Relevance

The evidence used in a text must be _____ to the author's _____ _____.

Using irrelevant or out-of-context _____ is a sign of an _____ text.

Relevant evidence is also _____.

Lesson Wrap-up

READING APPLICATION

Read the article excerpt titled *The Popularity of Glasses* that explores eye care in the United States. Pay close attention to the annotations.

What is the credible source cited in the excerpt?

Key Terms

Beside each definition, write the corresponding term.

_____: When information is as correct and unbiased as possible

_____: A long example told as a story

_____: The result of a logical argument

_____: What makes someone or something believable

_____: A piece of information, also called a supporting detail, which is used to support a main idea

_____: A specific instance or illustration that demonstrates a point

_____: An opinion or statement shared by someone who is knowledgeable about a topic

_____: A piece of information that most people generally agree to be true

_____: The thoughts or feelings of the author

_____: When information is clearly related to the text around it

_____: A number or percentage that represents research data

_____: A piece of information, also called evidence, that is used to support a main idea

Lesson 3.5
Understanding the Basics of Logic

OBJECTIVES

★ Recognize the difference between deductive and inductive logic.
★ Understand the basic principles of logic.

BIG IDEA

Understanding the basics of logic will help you use critical thinking to become a better reader and writer.

Logic is a method for carefully thinking through a topic to find a reasonable _____.

This lesson will focus on three basic elements of logic:

- Premises and Conclusions
- Inductive Reasoning
- Deductive Reasoning

Premises and Conclusions

Premises are two or more or more pieces of _____ that support a **logical argument**.

Example:

Premise 1: All men are mortal.
Premise 2: Socrates is a man.
Conclusion: Therefore, Socrates is mortal.

Because both premises in this argument are true, the conclusion is also true. This means that the argument itself is _____.

If one of the premises is false, the conclusion will also be _____.

Example:

Premise 1: All elephants can fly.
Premise 2: Robert is an elephant.
Conclusion: Robert can fly.

The conclusion is _____ because the first premise, *all elephants can fly*, is false.

READING APPLICATION

Read the paragraph *Who Needs Homework?* and pay close attention to the premises and conclusions. Then, answer the questions below.

What is the premise in the first sentence?

Lesson 3.5 | Understanding the Basics of Logic

What is the premise in the third sentence?

What is the logical conclusion?

On Your Own

Read the following argument and identify the false premise.

 _____ All bugs are poisonous.
 _____ A frog is not a bug.
 _____ Therefore, frogs are not poisonous.

After you complete the above exercise, try to rewrite the argument with true premises that yield a logical conclusion:

Premise 1:

Premise 2:

Conclusion:

Inductive Reasoning

Inductive reasoning uses _____ premises to reach a _____ conclusion.

Because inductive arguments use specific examples to make general conclusions, they can never claim that a conclusion is _____ _____.

Example:

  Premise 1: All my friends at college have taken a speech class.
  Premise 2: All the new students I've met on campus are in a speech class.
  Conclusion: Therefore, all the students at this college take speech classes.

Is this conclusion true? Why or why not?

The more evidence included in an inductive argument, the more logical its conclusion. By adding a _____ premise to the previous example, the inductive reasoning becomes even _____.

Example:

  Premise 1: All my friends at college have taken a speech class.
  Premise 2: All the new students I've met on campus are in a speech class.
  Premise 3: A speech class is a pre-requisite for most of the classes at this college.
  Conclusion: Therefore, all the students at this college probably take speech classes.

Deductive Reasoning

Deductive reasoning starts with a _____ premise and argues toward a _____ conclusion.

Example:

Premise 1: All the new students at this university must attend an orientation day.
Premise 2: Alfredo is a new student.
Conclusion: Alfredo must attend an orientation day.

Write the conclusion of the following deductive argument:

Premise 1: Each watermelon that goes though the checkout line must be scanned.
Premise 2: That watermelon will go through the checkout line.
Conclusion:

Because deductive arguments make claims about very _____ examples, their conclusions can be considered true if they follow these guidelines:

Deductive Reasoning Checklist

- ✓ All of the premises of the _____ must be _____.

- ✓ All of the premises must be _____ _____.

- ✓ No new _____ can be introduced into the _____.

Read the following example from the lesson.

Premise 1: Full-time city bus drivers make less than $20,000 a year.
Premise 2: Amanda is a full-time city bus driver.
Conclusion: Therefore, the city should raise the minimum wage to $15 an hour.

In this example, both of the premises are true and closely related; however, this is not a logical argument because the _____ introduces _____ _____.

Re-write the conclusion to make this argument logical.

Premise 1: Full-time city bus drivers make less than $20,000 a year.
Premise 2: Amanda is a full-time city bus driver.
Conclusion:

Lesson 3.5 | Understanding the Basics of Logic

READING APPLICATION

Read the essay titled *Our College Needs Expanded Daycare*. Pay close attention to the annotations when reading. Note how the author uses both inductive and deductive reasoning to support his claim. Then, answer the following questions.

What are the two premises provided in the first paragraph? What is the logical conclusion?

Premise 1:

Premise 2:

Conclusion:

What type of reasoning is the author using in Premise 1 of the first paragraph? *Hint: The argument begins with the <u>specific premise</u> that the college wishes to improve services for its students.*

☐ Inductive Reasoning ☐ Deductive Reasoning

What are the two premises provided in the second paragraph? What is the logical conclusion?

Premise 1:

Premise 2:

Conclusion:

Lesson Wrap-up

Key Terms

Define the following Key Terms from this lesson.

Conclusion:

Deductive Reasoning:

Inductive Reasoning:

Logic:

Logical Argument:

Premise:

Lesson 3.6
Recognizing Logical Fallacies

OBJECTIVE

★ Recognize common types of logical fallacies.

BIG IDEA

A **logical fallacy** is a faulty or incorrect argument. Being able to identify logical fallacies in a text will allow you to recognize weak and strong arguments.

When discovered, fallacies always make a text or presentation _____. All too often, however, fallacies appear so logical and persuasive that the audience accepts them as _____.

This is the goal of a fallacy:

This lesson will help you become familiar with the different types of logical fallacies.

READING APPLICATION

Read the passage titled *Mayor Wilson Should Resign*. See if you can spot faulty reasoning in this piece of writing. Then, answer the following questions.

What is the personal attack made against Mayor Wilson?

What does the author of the letter say the city has been doing successfully for 100 years?

What does the author say will happen if city buses are replaced with trolleys? Does this seem logical?

What evidence from the radio show does the author use? Does this effectively support the argument?

Types of Fallacies

Ad Hominem

Ad hominem arguments attack a person's _____ or _____ instead of examining her actual position.

Appeal to Tradition
An **appeal to tradition** argues that something is _____ simply because it has _____ been done that way.

Bandwagon
A **bandwagon** fallacy claims that something is _____ because many people are _____ _____.

Devil Words
Devil words are _____ that stir up _____ emotions in an audience.

False Authority
False authority claims that a person's _____ gives him or her _____ on a topic, even if the discussion is completely _____ to that person's area of expertise.

Hasty Generalization
A **hasty generalization** bases an argument about a _____ group on evidence from a _____ group.

Post Hoc
A *post hoc* fallacy _____ that one event _____ a second, completely _____ event.

Straw Man
A **straw man** fallacy _____ an opponent's _____ to make it easier to _____.

READING APPLICATION

Read the blog post *Your Food is Killing Me!* and ask yourself if the author is a trustworthy source; then, answer the questions below.

Do you think the writer of this blog post is qualified to write about diet and health? Why or why not?

What is the *ad hominem* argument this writer makes against Paula Deen?

What devil words does the author use in paragraph 2?

What *post hoc* fallacy does the author use?

Finding Fallacies

To find potential fallacies in a text or presentation, you must first carefully _____ the author's _____.

List the four questions you can use to analyze an author's argument:

1.   3.

2.   4.

On Your Own

Read the following excerpt and identify a sentence that contains a logical fallacy.

> The impersonal nature of the internet is one major cause of cyber-bullying. When communicating online, teenagers are more comfortable than they would be in a face-to-face conversation. Research by psychologist Rhonda Peters shows that "typing words on a keyboard feels very different than actually saying them to someone's face" (54). This can lead some young people to write cruel things online that they would never say in person.
>
> Helping teenagers think about the person "behind the screen" can teach them that their words have hurtful, often tragic consequences. According to a survey of thirteen students at McKinley High School, discussing real-life stories of cyber-bullying makes young people less likely to post cruel comments about others online. The results of this survey show that using a similar strategy would greatly reduce cyber-bullying at schools across America.

Lesson Wrap-up

Key Terms

Write the number of each fallacy next to its corresponding example.

1. *Ad Hominem*
2. Appeal to Tradition
3. Bandwagon
4. Devil Words
5. False Authority
6. Hasty Generalization
7. *Post Hoc*
8. Straw Man

_____ That politician doesn't agree with a lot of people on some issues. He must be a fascist.

_____ Mike should not be class president because he always submits his homework late.

_____ My favorite football star, John Jones, is in a commercial for that new cereal that helps you run faster and lose weight.

_____ The researcher who said it's best to have three recesses per day doesn't want our kids to have enough time in class.

_____ We have always played that song during games, so we should not discontinue it.

_____ The principal said that the students could no longer have early dismissal on Fridays because there has been a lot of vandalism in the town lately.

_____ All the cities near us have begun to make recycling mandatory. We should do the same thing.

_____ Ten children got sick from this vaccine, so it should be banned nationwide.

Lesson 3.7
Analyzing and Evaluating Visuals

OBJECTIVE

★ Understand how to analyze visuals.

BIG IDEA

Learning to evaluate images is an essential critical thinking skill. Once you are able to interpret the meaning of a photo or video, you can decide how you want to respond.

In this lesson, you will learn how to evaluate three aspects of images:

- Purpose
- Composition
- Argument

Purpose

To start _____ an image, you must first think about its _____. Just like texts, images can _____, _____, _____, or _____. Often, the purpose of an image is made clear through _____: how and when the image is presented to the viewer.

Composition

Composition: how the contents of an image have been _____ and _____. In some instances, composition choices are used to _____ or _____.

Emphasizing or including certain details isn't necessarily dishonest. It's important to remember, however, that images are not "_____." Anytime you analyze photos or videos, you need to consider how _____ affects the way you _____ their _____.

READING APPLICATION

Examine the photograph of the office environment. Then, read the analysis below it.

How might the photo's purpose change if it included a cluttered desk, dim lighting, and frowning people?

Argument

All images make some kind of **argument**. Even _____ photos and videos must _____ for your _____ and _____.

What are the three types of argumentation strategies?

1.

2.

3.

Ethos

Ethos: an argument based on _____. Images can be used to add _____ to a _____.

Logos

Logos: an argument based on _____. Advertisements often use _____-and-_____ photos to prove that a certain product will give the promised results. *Logos* can also be established by showing just the _____ of an action or event.

Pathos

Pathos: an argument based on _____. Images are often the easiest way to _____ the _____ of viewers. Images that use too much *pathos* can become emotionally _____.

List the four questions you can use to evaluate the strength of an image's argument:

1.   3.

2.   4.

READING APPLICATION

Study the image of the billboard advertisement. Then, read the visual analysis underneath it.

Describe the composition of the visual:

What do you suppose is the purpose?

What is the context of the visual?

On Your Own

Think about the photograph below. How do purpose, composition, and argument affect the way you understand and interpret this image? In the space below, write your interpretation of the image and which argumentation strategies you think it uses.

Lesson Wrap-up

Key Terms

Write the number of each term next to its definition.

1. *Ethos*
2. *Purpose*
3. *Composition*
4. *Context*
5. *Credibility*
6. *Logos*
7. *Pathos*

_____ How the contents of an image have been selected and arranged

_____ How and when information is presented

_____ What makes someone or something believable

_____ An argument based on a person's credibility

_____ An argument based on logic

_____ An argument based on emotion

_____ The goal of an image

Define the following Key Terms from this lesson.

Argument:

Entertaining Text:

Informative Text:

Persuasive Text:

Reflective Text:

Chapter 4
Grammar and Mechanics

Lesson 4.1
Understanding Nouns

OBJECTIVES

- ★ Define and locate nouns.
- ★ Distinguish between different types of nouns.
- ★ Recognize different functions of nouns in a sentence.

BIG IDEA

A noun is a part of speech that represents a person, place, thing, event, or idea; the English language is full of them, and without them, you wouldn't be able to talk about much.

Fill in the table with your own examples of nouns:

People	Places	Things	Events	Ideas

In this lesson, you will learn about the following:

- Common and Proper Nouns
- Singular and Plural Nouns
- Count and Non-Count Nouns
- Compound Nouns
- The Functions of Nouns

Lesson 4.1 | Understanding Nouns

On Your Own

Read the following paragraph and identify a noun.

> Africa has seen many great leaders, but none have been as influential as Nelson Mandela. He fought against Apartheid, a political revolution that violently divided people by race. Mandela is best known for serving time in jail as a result of political protesting. The country mourned his death when he passed in South Africa in 2013.

Common and Proper Nouns

Proper nouns are the names of _____ people, places, things, events, or ideas.

Common nouns name _____ people, places, things, events, or ideas. Because these nouns are general, they do _____ start with a capital letter unless they are located at the beginning of a sentence.

On Your Own

In the table below, use the list of common nouns to create your own list of proper nouns. For example, for the common noun *city*, you could write *Seattle* or *Budapest*. Write your ideas in the spaces provided.

Common Nouns	Proper Nouns
author	
activist	
friend	
state	
school	
website	
dog	

Singular and Plural Nouns

Singular nouns refer to _____ person, place, thing, event, or idea. **Plural nouns** refer to _____ people, places, things, events, or ideas.

Complete the following table with your own examples of common, proper, singular, and plural nouns.

Common Nouns	Proper Nouns	Singular Nouns	Plural Nouns
College	Baylor University	Canada	countries

Count and Non-Count Nouns

Count nouns are nouns that can be _____. **Non-count nouns** are nouns that can't be _____.

Which of the following examples are count and which are non-count? Write "count" or "non-count" in the table below.

three mails	
three Targets	
three electricities	
three concerts	

Compound Nouns

Some nouns are made up of more than one word. These are known as _____ _____.

Some compound nouns are joined together into one word while some are separated by _____ or _____.

The Function of Nouns

Subject

Nouns can be used in several basic ways. First, they can act as the **subject** of a sentence. The subject of a sentence is simply _____ or _____ the sentence is about.

Lesson 4.1 | Understanding Nouns

Grammar Practice 1

Identify the noun acting as the subject in each sentence. Check your work using the Answer Key in the back of the book.

One lucky student will win this awesome bike.

My sister always gets good grades.

Add a subject to each sentence:

My _____ called me last night at 11:00.

Several _____ crossed the road in front of me.

Direct Object

A **direct object** receives the action of a **verb**.

Grammar Practice 2

Identify the direct object in each sentence. Check your work using the Answer Key in the back of the book.

The chicken ate a bug.

The farmer planted his crops.

Object of a Preposition

The **object of a preposition** is the noun that completes a _____ _____.

(Prepositions show location, direction, or time.)

Grammar Practice 3

Identify the noun acting as an object of a preposition in each of the following sentences. Check your work using the Answer Key in the back of the book.

My nephew hid under the table and wanted me to find him.

We went down the river and swam in the deep water.

Adjectives

Nouns can act like **adjectives**, describing other _____ or _____.

Grammar Practice 4

Identify the noun that is acting as an adjective. Check your work using the Answer Key in the back of the book.

The mail truck has arrived!

I can't believe the cat knocked over his own food bowl.

Lesson Wrap-up

Key Terms

Define the Key Terms from this lesson.

Adjective:

Common Noun:

Compound Noun:

Count Noun:

Direct Object:

Hyphen:

Non-count Noun:

Noun:

Object of a Preposition:

Plural Noun:

Prepositional Phrase:

Proper Noun:

Singular Noun:

Subject:

Verb:

Lesson 4.2
Understanding Pronouns

OBJECTIVES

- ★ Connect pronouns and antecedents.
- ★ Define and identify personal, relative, and indefinite pronouns.
- ★ Identify subjective, objective, and possessive pronouns.
- ★ Locate and classify personal pronouns by person, gender, number, and case.
- ★ Recognize indefinite, personal, and relative pronouns in sentences.

BIG IDEA

A pronoun is a word that takes the place of a noun in a sentence and can represent people, places, things, events, or ideas. Understanding and utilizing pronouns helps you avoid repeating the same word over and over again in the same piece of writing.

In this lesson, you will learn about three important types of pronouns:

- Personal Pronouns
- Indefinite Pronouns
- Relative Pronouns

Personal Pronouns

Personal pronouns are the most common type of pronoun. They rename specific _____, _____, _____, or _____. Personal pronouns change _____ depending on how they are used in a sentence.

Pronouns can be categorized in four ways:

1.

2.

3.

4.

Grammar Practice 1

Identify all the personal pronouns in the sentences below. Check your work using the Answer Key in the back of the book.

After soccer practice, I made sure to drink plenty of water.

You aren't really a true Jacksonville Jaguars fan unless you get upset when they lose!

Personal Pronouns   103

Number: Plural and Singular Pronouns

In grammar, **number** refers to whether a word is singular or plural.

When pronouns are divided by number, they are separated into two groups: _____ and _____. **Singular pronouns** refer to one person or object while **plural pronouns** refer to multiple people or objects.

Grammar Practice 2

Locate the pronouns provided for each of the following sentences. Check your work using the Answer Key in the back of the book.

Identify all the singular pronouns in the following sentence:

> I was in the middle of cooking steak and potatoes when my friend invited me out to dinner.

Identify all the plural pronouns in the following sentence:

> The group decided that we would go for a walk after dinner; our stomachs needed help digesting.

An _____ is the word a pronoun renames in a sentence.

- If the antecedent of a pronoun is singular, the pronoun must be _____.

- If the antecedent of a pronoun is plural, the pronoun must be _____.

Person: First-, Second-, and Third-Person Pronouns

A second way to categorize pronouns is by _____: first, second, or third.

Use **first-person pronouns** when talking about _____.

Example:

> I walked alone.

Use **second-person** pronouns when talking directly to _____.

Example:

> Will you come with me?

Use **third-person** pronouns for _____.

Example:

> She is coming with us.

Grammar Practice 3

In the sentences below, identify the pronouns based on their category. Check your work using the Answer Key in the back of the book.

First Person

What is up with me these days? I have been so scatterbrained lately that my friends are concerned.

Second Person

What are your plans later on today? If you would like, we can go shopping.

Third Person

She has been doing such a great job at work that they have promoted her to manager.

Gender: Male, Female, and Neutral Pronoun Genders

The third way to categorize pronouns is by _____. There are three genders in the English language: _____, _____, and _____. Only third-person pronouns are specific to gender.

Male gender pronouns:

Female gender pronouns:

Neutral gender pronouns:

Grammar Practice 4

Complete the following sentences with the correct pronoun. The gender of the pronoun should match the noun it renames. Check your work using the Answer Key in the back of the book.

Franco washed _____ car.

Cindy said that the coat belongs to _____ .

Our neighbors invited us to _____ house for dinner.

Case: Subjective-, Objective-, and Possessive-Case Pronouns

Subjective-case pronouns are used as the _____ of a _____.

Objective-case pronouns are used as objects of _____, _____, or _____. **Possessive-case pronouns** are used as _____ _____.

Grammar Practice 5

Complete each sentence with the correct pronoun(s). Check your work using the Answer Key in the back of the book.

That is _____ car.	(Possessive-case pronoun)

Indefinite Pronouns   105

Will you come to the movies with mom and _____?	(Objective-case pronoun)
_____ went to the store for me.	(Subjective-case pronoun)
_____ car is parked in _____ parking space.	(Two possessive-case pronouns)
I threw the ball to _____ .	(Objective-case pronoun)

Indefinite Pronouns

Indefinite pronouns are pronouns that don't _____ a _____ _____. They can be divided into three groups: _____, _____, or _____.

Make a list of eight indefinite pronouns:

1.   5.

2.   6.

3.   7.

4.   8.

Relative Pronouns

Relative pronouns are used to _____ **dependent clauses**, groups of words with a subject and a **verb** that do not _____ a complete _____.

List the seven relative pronouns:

1.   5.

2.   6.

3.   7.

4.

Grammar Practice 6

Identify the relative pronouns in the sentence below. Check your work using the Answer Key in the back of the book.

> At the time of the election, many people were unhappy with both candidates, which led to political unrest.

Case

_____ and _____ are the only relative pronouns that have a specific case. *Who* is a _____-case pronoun and *whom* is an _____-case pronoun.

When deciding which one to use, you should determine how the pronoun is being used in the sentence. Try substituting the relative pronoun with a personal pronoun:

Subjective Case

Who is going to the park?

> She is going to the park.

Objective Case

Rhonda went to the museum with whom?

> Rhonda went to the museum with him.

Pronouns in Sentences

Pronoun Reference

When used in sentences, pronouns *refer* to _____ or other _____. This **reference** should be clear.

Here's an example of *unclear* reference:

> They have been working on them for a while, and they should be done by the end of the day.

If the scenario is talking about employees getting their résumés updated, how can you edit the sentence for clearer pronoun reference? Re-write the sentence below.

Pronouns and Antecedents

An antecedent is a _____ that indicates the specific person, place, thing, event, or idea a pronoun renames. Pronouns must agree with their antecedents in _____, _____, and _____.

Lesson Wrap-up

Test Yourself

Identify the pronouns in the following sentences and indicate their cases (subjective, objective, or possessive). Also indicate whether each pronoun is indefinite or relative. Check your work using the Answer Key in the back of the book.

1. Whenever I feel sad, I listen to my favorite music.

2. They are coming with you and me to the party.

3. Did you go to their house for Thanksgiving dinner?

4. My sister made up a game that was too difficult to play.

5. Please tell whomever is on the phone to call back later.

Key Terms

Define the following Key Terms from this lesson.

Adjective:

Antecedent:

Dependent Clause:

Direct Object:

First-person Pronoun:

Gender:

Indefinite Pronoun:

Indirect Object:

Noun:

Number:

Object of a Preposition:

Person:

Personal Pronoun:

Pronoun:

Pronoun-Antecedent Agreement:

Pronoun Case:

Pronoun Reference:

Relative Pronoun:

Second-person Pronoun:

Subject:

Third-person Pronoun:

Verb:

Lesson 4.3
Understanding Verbs

OBJECTIVES

★ Identify irregular future-tense verbs.
★ Identify the characteristics and purposes of verbs.
★ Recognize action verbs, helping verbs, and linking verbs.
★ Recognize and understand how to form past-, present-, and future-tense verbs.
★ Identify regular and irregular verbs.
★ Recognize past and present participles.
★ Recognize the past-perfect, present-perfect, and future-perfect tenses.

BIG IDEA

Verbs are words that represent actions, relationships, or states of being. Verbs are an essential part of every sentence, and it would be impossible to communicate without verbs, which hold everything together.

In this lesson, you will learn about verb types and tenses:

- Verb Types
- Simple Tenses
- Verb Forms

Verb Types

Action Verbs

Action verbs show _____ or _____ _____.

Example:

On her birthday, Stella opened her presents with joy.

Direct & Indirect Objects

Sometimes, an action verb is followed by a _____ _____, a word that receives the action of the verb.

Example:

Gina accidentally *baked* the pie for too long.

An **indirect object** is a word that receives the direct object.

Example:

After the semester, the professor *gave* Alonzo a **letter** of recommendation for all his hard work.

Linking Verbs

Linking verbs link the _____ to a _____.

Lesson 4.3 | Understanding Verbs

List eight examples of linking verbs:

1.   5.

2.   6.

3.   7.

4.   8.

Linking Verbs vs Action Verbs

There are some linking verbs that can also function as action verbs. To determine which way they are used, you should _____ the _____ of the sentence.

Examples:

Darla tasted the food.

The food tasted awful.

List ten words that commonly function as both action and linking verbs:

1.   6.

2.   7.

3.   8.

4.   9.

5.   10.

Helping Verbs

The **main verb** is the verb that expresses the primary action or state of being in a complete sentence.

Helping verbs are added to a main verb to create a new verb that grammatically fits the sentence.

Example:

Jenny has completed all training in preparation for next month's marathon.

In this sentence, the helping verb *has* is helping the main verb *completed*.

Helping Verbs vs Linking Verbs

Some helping verbs can also be used as both helping verbs and linking verbs.

Examples:

The lifeguard was watching the beachgoers during his entire shift.

In this sentence, the verb _____ is helping the main verb, _____.

The lifeguard was happy to be off work after a long day in the sun.

In this sentence, the verb *was* is linking the subject, _____, to its description: _____.

On Your Own

Read the following paragraph and identify a helping verb.

The marketing company was using both online and offline strategies to reach its audience. Usually, this audience is unified by a common interest or goal, not by the corporation itself. Because the company was planning events, promotions, and contests, the audience was more trusting. This type of marketing is often wildly successful; in many instances, the company even encourages new product development for the corporation.

Grammar Practice 1

Fill in the blanks with a helping verb to make the sentence grammatically correct. Check your work using the Answer Key in the back of the book.

She _____ take piano lessons next year.

I _____ going to the mall.

Simple Verb Tenses

Verbs also have _____ that let the reader know *when* an action is taking place. The most common tenses are _____ tense, _____ tense, and _____ tense.

Past Tense

Past tense is used to report an event or reflect on a _____ experience. The writer uses past tense to let the reader know that the action is over.

Examples:

Past-tense action verb:

Frederick borrowed his brother's iPhone charger yesterday.

Past-tense helping verb:

Jamie was uninterested in eating meat after watching a documentary on animal cruelty.

Past-tense action verb (with helping verb):

Stanley was walking to work.

Regular vs Irregular Verbs

With regular verbs, the past tense is formed by _____ -ed (or -d if the verb ends in e) to the end of the base form of the verb.

Example:

I listened to my professor talk about the Civil War last week.

Irregular verbs have unique patterns and can completely change form in the past tense.

Example:

Ryan drove his mother to the airport yesterday.

On Your Own

Identify a past-tense verb in the following paragraph.

Cheryl was going to go to the store after work, but the storm stopped her. Before she knew it, all kinds of debris went flying past her office window. Hail rained down on her car parked just ten feet away, and garbage from the nearby trashcan stuck to its window. She was glad Jennifer had stopped her to discuss the meeting next week, or she would have been caught in that storm!

Present Tense

When writing about events or actions that are happening _____, you should use the **present tense**.

Examples:

Present-tense action verb:

Alyssa watches her German Shepherd play at the dog park.

Present-tense linking verb:

The new restaurant is affordable.

Present-tense action verb (with helping verb):

Westley is thinking he might get into law school next year.

On Your Own

Read the following paragraph and identify a present-tense verb.

The air is frigid, and my hands are numb. I think even the snow foxes are huddled together for warmth. This morning was warmer, but now I am sure the temperature has dropped at least fifteen degrees. My dog stays close to my side and whines to find warmth and shelter. The sun is starting to break through the clouds, but somehow it seems colder than it was before.

Future Tense

The **future tense** is used to describe events or actions that have not yet _____ _____ or to describe plans or instructions.

Example:
Future-tense linking verb:

This living room will look incredible once it is furnished.

On Your Own

Read the following paragraph and identify a future-tense verb.

One day, she will look up and see just how far she has come. She will realize that everything has been building to this moment. She will gaze out over the crowd of people cheering her name, and the weight of ten years' hard work will disappear.

Verb Forms & Functions

The **base form** of a verb is the _____ form of a verb. The base form can be _____ or _____ to create **verbals**: _____.

There are three types of verbals:

1.
2.
3.

Infinitives

The word *to* + the base form creates the **infinitive**: a verbal that can function as a noun, adjective, or adverb in a sentence. Infinitives are often used to reference expectations or intentions.

Example:

Remind me not to forget my water bottle when we leave the gym.

Gerunds

Gerunds function as nouns and are formed by adding *–ing* to the base form of a verb.

Example:

Diving is Jenna's favorite sport to watch.

Past Participles

The **past participle** is a verb form used to show completed mental or physical action. Past participles can function as adjectives that express an action or a state of being.

Lesson 4.3 | Understanding Verbs

Example:

Dale the dog was <u>excited</u> to receive a treat after a long day of being a good boy.

Regular vs Irregular Past Participles

A regular past participle is formed by adding *-ed* (or just *-d* if the verb ends in *e*) to the end of a regular verb. Irregular verbs change completely to form their past participles.

What is the regular past participle of the verb *walk*?

What is the irregular past participle of the verb *catch*?

Present Participles

A present participle is formed by adding *-ing* to the _____ of the base form of a verb.

Present participles can function in two ways:

1.
2.

On Your Own

Practice forming present participles with the following verbs by filling in the blank column. The first example has been completed for you.

Base Form	Present Participle
cook	cooking
smell	
write	
break	
sing	

Perfect & Progressive Tenses

Perfect Tenses

Past-Perfect Tense

The **past-perfect tense** is used to describe a _____ action that was _____ before another past-completed action.

Example:

Amanda <u>had driven</u> forty miles before she realized she forgot her purse at home.

Perfect & Progressive Tenses 115

Present-Perfect Tense

The **present-perfect tense** is used to describe:

It is formed by combining the correct form of the helping verb *have* with a verb's _____ _____.

Future-Perfect Tense

The **future-perfect tense** _____ an _____ that will be completed before another _____ event. It is formed by _____ *will have* with the past participle of a _____.

On Your Own

Read the following sentences and choose the box to indicate whether the sentence is in past-perfect tense, present-perfect tense, or future-perfect tense.

Shelia has worked hard over the past fifteen years.

☐ Past-perfect tense
☐ Present-perfect tense
☐ Future-perfect tense

Alyssa had tried to talk to Marion several times before.

☐ Past-perfect tense
☐ Present-perfect tense
☐ Future-perfect tense

I will have watched ten movies by the end of spring break.

☐ Past-perfect tense
☐ Present-perfect tense
☐ Future-perfect tense

Progressive Tenses

Past-Progressive Tense

The **past-progressive tense** is used to describe actions that meet 1 of 3 criteria:

1. actions that were already in progress in the past

2.

3.

The past-progressive tense is formed by using the past-tense form of the verb *be* with the present participle of a verb.

Example:

I was cleaning the kitchen when my friend came over for coffee.

Lesson 4.3 | Understanding Verbs

Present-Progressive Tenses

The **present-progressive tense** is used to do 1 of 3 things:

1. describe a _____ action,
2. discuss an on-going action happening in the _____,
3. or describe an event that will happen in the _____ _____.

It is formed using the present-tense form of the verb *be* and the present participle of a verb.

Example:

The chefs <u>are</u> <u>preparing</u> the buffet dinner for tonight's event.

Future-Progressive Tense

The **future-progressive tense** is used to describe _____ that _____ happen in the _____. It is formed by combining the verb phrase *will be* and the _____ _____ of the verb.

Example:

Beyoncé <u>will</u> <u>be</u> <u>headlining</u> after the opening artist performs.

On Your Own

Identify the present participle in each of the following sentences. Then, check the box next to the correct tense.

The storm is going to be intense this weekend.

☐ Past-progressive tense
☐ Present-progressive tense
☐ Future-progressive tense

She was eating her dinner when the call came in.

☐ Past-progressive tense
☐ Present-progressive tense
☐ Future-progressive tense

I will be studying that chapter tonight.

☐ Past-progressive tense
☐ Present-progressive tense
☐ Future-progressive tense

Lesson Wrap-up

Key Terms

Define the following Key Terms from this lesson.

Action Verb:

Lesson Wrap-up

Base Form:

Direct Object:

Future Tense:

Future-perfect Tense:

Gerund:

Helping Verb:

Helping Verb:

Indirect Object:

Infinitive:

Linking Verb:

Main Verb:

Participle Phrase:

Past Participle:

Past Tense:

Past-perfect Tense:

Past-progressive Tense:

Prepositional Phrase:

Present Participle:

Present Tense:

Present-perfect Tense:

Present-progressive Tense:

Subject:

Verb:

Verbal:

Lesson 4.4
Understanding Adjectives and Adverbs

OBJECTIVE

★ Understand the characteristics and purposes of adjectives and adverbs.

BIG IDEA

Adjectives and adverbs are especially helpful for giving descriptions and adding detail.

In this lesson, you will learn about:

- Forms and Functions of Adjectives
- Forms and Functions of Adverbs

Forms and Functions of Adjectives

Adjectives are used to describe _____ or _____. Adjectives answer these five questions:

1.

2.

3.

4.

5.

Example:

Sama bought a <u>beautiful</u> <u>purple</u> dress and <u>three</u> necklaces.

When an adjective is used to compare items, its form changes.

When you are comparing two items, follow this rule:

Examples:

Rachel is <u>taller</u> than anyone else in the class.
Nathaniel was a <u>more finicky</u> eater than his brother.

When you are comparing more than two items, follow this rule:

Examples:

Rachel is the <u>tallest</u> person in her class.
He is the <u>most ambitious</u> business owner I know.

On Your Own

Identify the adjectives (excluding articles) in the following sentences:

The play expertly portrays the complicated and intricate web of relationships.

We have just received your letter concerning the upcoming publication of your new novel.

This article thoroughly examines the role of technology in strong reading and writing skills.

Forms and Functions of Adverbs

Adverbs answer these five questions:

1.

2.

3.

4.

5.

Adverbs describe _____, _____, and _____ _____. The most common type of adverb describes a verb and ends in -_____.

Examples:

Richard <u>happily</u> skipped to his car after their date.
Dante was working <u>tirelessly</u> to complete his end-of-the-year project.

Grammar Practice 1

Identify the adverb in each sentence. Check your work using the Answer Key in the back of the book.

The elderly man limped painfully after his surgery.

I shop at that store often.

Mom hid her jewelry carefully.

Adverbs also describe adjectives and other adverbs.

Adjectives

Apparently, the new horror movie coming out is <u>more</u> terrifying than the last one.

Adverbs

Cats can't really be trained, but mine responds to his name <u>very</u> well.

Just like adjectives, adverbs can be used to make _____. To compare two actions with an adverb, follow this rule:

On Your Own

Read the following sentences and identify adverbs.

The play expertly portrays the complicated and intricate web of family relationships.

We have just received your letter concerning the upcoming publication of your new novel.

This article thoroughly examines the role of technology in strong reading and writing skills.

Lesson Wrap-up

Key Terms

Define the Key Terms from this lesson.

Adjective:

Adverb:

Article:

Linking Verb:

Noun:

Pronoun:

Lesson 4.5
Understanding Prepositions

OBJECTIVE

★ Understand the characteristics and purposes of prepositions.

BIG IDEA

Prepositions are words that show relationships among people, places, things, events, and ideas.

In this lesson, you will learn about:

- Purposes and Functions of Common Prepositions
- Purposes and Functions of Prepositional Phrases

Purposes and Functions of Common Prepositions

Prepositions are words that show _____ among the words in a _____. Sometimes, these _____ are _____ _____.

Grammar Practice 1

Fill in the blanks with a preposition that shows location. Check your work using the Answer Key in the back of the book.

We took a ride _____ the boat.
We went _____ the opera house.
Sarah met her friends _____ the park.

Prepositions can also show relationships such as time. Fill in the blanks with a preposition that shows time:

Please have dinner ready _____ 6:00.
I drank a tall glass of water _____ the game.
I haven't seen her _____ eighth grade.

List 25 of the most common prepositions:

Lesson 4.5 | Understanding Prepositions

Purposes and Functions of Prepositional Phrases

Prepositions are always used to introduce a _____ _____. **Prepositional phrases** are _____ of _____ words that begin with a preposition and end with a noun or pronoun. The noun or pronoun that ends a prepositional phrase is known as the _____ of the preposition.

Example:

There was a spider <u>in my bedroom</u>, so I slept <u>on the couch</u>.

In a sentence, prepositional phrases usually function as either _____ or _____.

Prepositional Phrases as Adjectives

If a prepositional phrase is an adjective, it _____ a _____ or _____ and answers several questions.

Write the five questions that a prepositional phrase being used as an adjective will answer:

1.
2.
3.
4.
5.

Example:

In the forest, I found the most interesting flower <u>with two stems</u>.

On Your Own

Read the sentence and select the prepositional phrase acting as an adjective.

I went to the office so that I could borrow that important file of Jimmy's.

Prepositional Phrases as Adverbs

A prepositional phrase that is acting as an adverb will describe a _____ and answer one of the following questions:

1.
2.

3.

4.

5.

Example:

Angelica biked to the grocery store for ice cream.

In this sentence, there are two prepositional phrases acting as adverbs. The first one, *to the grocery store*, describes _____ Angelica went. The second one, *for ice cream*, shows _____ Angelica went.

Lesson Wrap-up

Key Terms

Match each Key Term with its definition.

A. Object of the Preposition
B. Adverb
C. Pronoun
D. Prepositional Phrase
E. Noun
F. Adjective
G. Preposition
H. Subject
I. Verb

_____ A word that describes a noun or pronoun

_____ A word that describes a verb, adjective, or another adverb

_____ A word that represents a person, place, thing, or idea

_____ A word that completes the meaning of a preposition in a prepositional phrase

_____ A word that takes the place of a noun in a sentence

_____ A word that shows a relationship among people, places, things, events, and ideas

_____ A group of related words that starts with a preposition and ends with a noun or pronoun

_____ The person, place, thing, event, or idea a sentence is about

_____ A word that represents an action, relationship, or state of being

Lesson 4.6
Understanding Clauses and Conjunctions

OBJECTIVES

- ★ Recognize independent and dependent clauses.
- ★ Define and identify different types of conjunctions.
- ★ Recognize coordinating, correlative, and subordinating conjunctions.

BIG IDEA

Your writing will become smoother and easier to read when you utilize clauses and conjunctions to join ideas together in a logical way.

In this lesson, you will learn about forming simple, compound, complex, and compound-complex sentences with the following components:

- Related Words and Clause
- Coordinating Conjunctions
- Subordinating Conjunctions
- Correlative Conjunctions
- Conjunctive Adverbs

Related Words and Clauses

A **simple sentence** includes the following 3 elements:

1.

2.

3.

Clauses

A **clause** is a word group containing a _____ and a _____. An **independent clause** can stand alone as a _____ _____. A **dependent clause** is a word group containing a _____ and a _____ that cannot stand alone as a complete sentence.

Sentence Patterns

List the combinations in each sentence pattern:

Simple Sentence	
Compound Sentence	

Coordinating Conjunctions   125

Complex Sentence	
Compound-Complex Sentence	

Define the term **conjunction**.

List the three main kinds of conjunctions:

1.

2.

3.

Coordinating Conjunctions

Coordinating conjunctions join similar _____ or _____ of words together.

List the 7 coordinating conjunctions:

F	
A	
N	
B	
O	
Y	
S	

Coordinating conjunctions can connect _____, _____, or _____ that carry equal weight in the sentence.

Words

The first function of coordinating conjunctions is joining two or more words, such as _____, _____, _____, or _____.

Nouns   Cecilia and Bea were eager to compete against each other.

Adjectives	During the tour, we saw manatees in the <u>clear</u> and <u>sparkling</u> water.
Adverbs	The oak tree's leaves fell <u>suddenly</u> and <u>unexpectedly</u> only two weeks into autumn.
Verbs	The results of the study both <u>surprised</u> and <u>worried</u> the team of scientists.

Phrases

Coordinating conjunctions can also be used to join whole phrases, such as _____ _____.

Example:

The deer quickly jumped <u>into the backyard</u> **and** <u>over the fence</u>.

Clauses

Finally, coordinating conjunctions help form compound sentences. A **compound sentence** is a sentence pattern in which two _____ _____ are connected by a **comma** and a coordinating conjunction.

Example:

<u>She couldn't make it to the concert</u>, **so** <u>she went to the park instead</u>.

On Your Own

Read the following passage and identify a coordinating conjunction.

> Every day, Mary and Susan leave their houses, and they walk to school together. The neighbor's dog usually follows them, but today he was nowhere to be found. Susan wondered if the dog was sick, so before they went to school, they stopped at the neighbor's house. The dog poked his nose out when his owner answered the door, and the girls smiled as they went off in the direction of the school.

Subordinating Conjunctions

Subordinating conjunctions introduce dependent clauses. A dependent clause can join an independent clause to form a _____ _____.

List 10 common subordinating conjunctions:

1.
2.
3.
4.
5.
6.
7.
8.
9.
10.

On Your Own

Read the following passage and identify a subordinating conjunction.

> While Sara was doing the dishes, she heard a knock on her door. She went to answer it even though she wasn't expecting anyone. When she opened the door, a cat peered up at her. It looked hungry and dirty and had, apparently, learned to knock. It wasn't until Sara stepped outside that she saw the pot that the cat had been rubbing against to knock on the door.

Correlative Conjunctions

Correlative conjunctions are similar to _____ _____; they both connect two or more word groups of _____ _____. Correlative conjunctions always appear in _____.

Write the five correlative conjunction pairs:

1.
2.
3.
4.
5.

Correlative Conjunctions and Subject-Verb Agreement

When using *both/and* to join subjects in a sentence, make sure you use a _____ verb. When using *either/or* to join subjects in a sentence, make sure the verb agrees with the subject _____ to it.

On Your Own

Read the following passage and identify the sentence that uses correlative conjunctions.

> Seattle, Washington is appealing because it provides access to mountains and beaches. Downtown Seattle, including the famous Pike Place Market, is right on the water.

Originally, Pike Place was a fish market. Today, it's a maze of both indoor and outdoor shops. These shops sell everything from spices to flower bouquets, and of course fresh seafood. There are also delicious restaurants and cafés in this area. However, if you visit Pike Place, be prepared for a crowd.

Conjunctive Adverbs

Like conjunctions, **conjunctive adverbs** are used to show _____, _____, _____, and other relationships between clauses.

Two closely-related independent clauses can be connected by a **semicolon**. To emphasize the relationship between the two clauses, a conjunctive adverb can be inserted after the semicolon that joins two closely-related independent clauses.

Add a conjunctive adverb to the following sentence:

Get your chores done; if you don't, you won't be able to go to the beach.

Test Yourself

Follow the instructions to select the appropriate type of conjunctions. Check your work using the Answer Key in the back of the book.

Identify the coordinating conjunctions in the following sentences:

1. I wanted ham, but we didn't have any, so we went out to eat instead.

2. We had ice cream and cake at the birthday party, but not everybody wanted some.

3. He and I will be getting married next year, so we have started planning now.

Identify the subordinating conjunctions in the following sentences:

4. Ever since I started exercising, I have felt a lot better.

5. After snacking all day, I couldn't eat dinner.

6. In spite of our differences, we have remained friends since first grade.

Identify the coordinating conjunctions that are joining two prepositional phrases:

7. We went over the mountain and through the woods.

8. I went through the yard and into the house.

Lesson Wrap-up

Key Terms

Define the Key Terms from this lesson.

Adjective:

Adverb:

Clause:

Comma:

Comma Splice:

Complex Sentence:

Compound Sentence:

Compound-complex Sentence:

Conjunction:

Conjunctive Adverb:

Coordinating Conjunction:

Correlative Conjunctions:

Dependent Clause:

FANBOYS:

Independent Clause:

Main Verb:

Noun:

Predicate:

Prepositional Phrase:

Semicolon:

Sentence Patterns:

Subject:

Subordinating Conjunction:

Verb:

Visual Learning:

Lesson 4.7
Identifying the Characteristics of Sentences

OBJECTIVES

- ★ Identify the characteristics of complete sentences.
- ★ Understand the characteristics and purposes of dependent and independent clauses.
- ★ Understand the characteristics and purposes of interjections.
- ★ Understand the difference between dependent and independent clauses.
- ★ Recognize subjects and verbs in complete sentences.
- ★ Recognize dependent and independent clauses in sentences.

BIG IDEA

The ability to group words together in complete sentences is essential in meaningful communication.

In this lesson, you will learn about the following sentence components:

- Capitalization and Punctuation
- Parts of Speech
- Subject and Predicate
- Complete Thought

Capitalization and Punctuation

Complete sentences always start with a _____ _____ and end with a _____, a _____ _____, or a(n) _____ _____.

Period:

Question Mark:

Exclamation Point:

Direct question:

Indirect question:

Types of Statements

Declarative Sentence:

Interrogative Sentence:

Imperative Sentence:

Exclamatory Sentence:

Parts of Speech

Nouns and Pronouns

A **noun** is a word that represents a _____, _____, _____, _____, or _____.

A **pronoun** is a part of speech used to replace a _____ or another _____.

Classifying Nouns

Common Noun:

Proper Noun:

Count Noun:

Non-Count Noun:

Classifying Pronouns

Personal Pronoun:

Relative Pronoun:

Indefinite Pronoun:

On Your Own

Identify the nouns in the following sentences:

> Don, my boyfriend, does not want to go to dinner. He said he ate turkey right after he finished watching Modern Family.

Identify the pronouns in the following sentences:

> I told Dr. Lovell that it was your original work. He didn't believe me and said that your homework needs to be re-done.

Verbs

Verb Types

Action Verb:

Linking Verb:

Helping Verb:

Lesson 4.7 | Identifying the Characteristics of Sentences

Verb Tenses

Past-Tense Verb:

Present-Tense Verb:

Future-Tense Verb:

Adjectives and Adverbs

Adjectives are used to _____ _____ or _____.

Adverbs _____ _____, _____, or other _____.

Prepositions

Prepositions show _____ among _____, _____, _____, _____, and _____. Prepositional phrases are word groups made up of a _____ and the _____ of the preposition.

Conjunctions

A **conjunction** is a part of speech that _____ two or more _____, _____, or _____ in a sentence.

Coordinating Conjunction:

Subordinating Conjunction:

Correlative Conjunction:

Interjections

Interjections are _____ or short _____ of words that show _____ or _____.

Subject and Predicate

A complete sentence must _____ include a _____ and a _____.

Subject Nouns and Pronouns

Subjects are usually stated _____ as nouns or pronouns.

Write your own sentence with a subject noun:

Subject and Predicate 133

Write your own sentence with a subject pronoun:

Subject Placement

The subject does not always have to be the _____ word in the sentence.

Write your own example of a subject that is not the first word in the sentence:

Implied Subjects

Sentences giving the audience a _____ or _____ contain an **implied subject**.

Write your own sentence with an implied subject:

Compound Subjects

Subjects can also be compound. In these instances, the subjects are linked by _____.

Write your own sentence with a **compound subject**:

Subjects vs Objects

Although nouns and pronouns often function as subjects, they also often function as objects. When looking for the subject of a sentence, you can rule out the following types of _____:

1.

2.

3.

The function of a pronoun determines its **case**. There are three pronoun cases:

1.

2.

3.

Predicates

Like nouns and pronouns, verbs can take on a variety of forms that serve different purposes in sentences.

Word Groups

Remember that predicates are often made up of a _____ _____ + a _____ _____.

© HAWKES LEARNING

Lesson 4.7 | Identifying the Characteristics of Sentences

Write your own sentence with a predicate made up of a word group:

Compound Verbs

Write your own sentence with a compound predicate:

Verbs with Other Functions

Verbs can also be used as _____ or _____ in a sentence.

On Your Own

Identify the subject and the main verb in each of the following sentences.

A merchant ship finally rescued the survivors after six days at sea.

In laying the foundation of his essay, Bitzer makes a number of assumptions about rhetoric.

Burke was the author of the popular essay "Reflections on the Revolution in France."

Steps for Locating the Subject and Predicate

1.

2.

3.

Complete Thought

When a group of words expresses a **complete thought**, the group of words is _____ _____. If a group of words contains a subject and a verb but does not express a complete thought, it is known as a _____ _____.

On Your Own

Read the following paragraph and identify the incomplete sentence.

While the availability of electronic resources has opened up new opportunities for reducing the cost of education. In first-year composition classes, instructors are selecting electronic textbooks or course companion websites instead of traditional print textbooks. Educators, however, are still unsure about the advantages of either type of text. More research must be conducted to determine if different textbook formats help students learn more effectively.

Lesson Wrap-up

Test Yourself

In the following sentences, identify the subject(s) and add the correct punctuation. Check your work using the Answer Key in the back of the book.

Whenever the four of us go shopping, I always spend too much money

Did you know the man down the street who passed away

Marcus and Steve joined our group and helped us raise money

Every time you get behind the wheel of a car, put your seatbelt on

Ever since I first saw you, I have thought you looked like Steve Carrell

Key Terms

Beside each definition, write the corresponding term.

_____ : A sentence that communicates emotion or surprise

_____ : A word that describe a noun or a pronoun

_____ : A verb tense used to describe events or actions that have not yet taken place or to describe plans or instructions

_____ : The simplest form of a verb, free of alterations for tense, number, and point of view

_____ : A word that completes the meaning of a prepositional phrase

_____ : A word that takes the place of a noun in a sentence

_____ : A word group that contains a subject and a verb

_____ : A part of speech that describes a verb, adjective, or another adverb

_____ : A part of speech that connects two or more words, phrases, or clauses in a sentence

_____ : A punctuation mark that conveys emphasis or strong feeling

_____ : Conjunctions that connect two or more similar ideas and always appear in pairs

_____ : A sentence that makes a general statement that informs the reader

_____ : A word that receives the action of a verb

Lesson 4.7 | Identifying the Characteristics of Sentences

_____: A sentence that asks the audience a question and usually ends with a question mark

_____: A pronoun that functions as an object in a sentence

_____: A conjunction that connects words or word groups of equal importance in a sentence

_____: A pronoun used to refer to the speaker of the sentence

_____: When a group of words is logically finished

_____: A word that changes the form of the main verb so that it grammatically fits in the sentence

_____: A sentence that makes commands and often addresses the implied subject

_____: The subject of a sentence when the speaker is talking directly to the audience

_____: A pronoun that does not rename a specific noun

_____: A word group that contains a subject and a verb and expresses a complete thought

_____: A sentence that contains at least one subject and one predicate and expresses a complete thought

_____: A sentence that tells the audience about a question and usually ends with a period

_____: A word or group of words that adds emphasis or emotion

_____: A sentence that asks a question

_____: A verb that links the subject to a description

_____: The verb that expresses the primary action or state of being of a subject in a complete sentence

_____: A sentence made up of one independent clause

_____: The categories that classify each type of word found in a sentence

_____: A verb tense used to report on an event or reflect on a past experience

_____: A punctuation mark used to end sentences that make a statement or relay information

_____: A pronoun that renames a specific person, animal, object, or place

Lesson Wrap-up

_____: A pronoun that shows possession of another noun

_____: The part of the sentence that states what the subject is doing

_____: A word that receives the direct object

_____: A group of related words that starts with a preposition and ends with a noun or pronoun

_____: A word that shows a relationship among people, places, things, events, and ideas

_____: A punctuation mark used at the end of a sentence that asks a question

_____: The form a pronoun takes based on its function—subjective, objective, or possessive—in a sentence

_____: The person, place, thing, event, or idea a sentence is about

_____: The form of a pronoun that functions as the subject in a sentence

_____: A word that represents an action, relationship, or state of being

Lesson 4.8
Identifying Common Sentence Errors

OBJECTIVES

★ Apply strategies for correcting fused sentences.
★ Define and identify different types of sentence errors.
★ Distinguish between complete and incomplete sentences in writing.
★ Recognize fused sentences.
★ Recognize sentence comma splices in writing.
★ Recognize sentence fragments in writing.

BIG IDEA

Being able to identify and correct common writing mistakes will ensure that you are communicating your ideas in the best way possible.

This lesson will teach you how to recognize and fix two types of sentence errors:

- Fragments
- Run-on Sentences

Fragments

A **fragment** is a sentence error that occurs when the sentence doesn't express a _____ _____.

Phrases

Some fragments are **phrases**, which are:

List the two ways to correct these types of fragments:

1.

2.

Dependent Clauses

Another type of fragment is a _____ _____, which has a _____ and a _____ but does not express a complete thought.

Some dependent clauses can be made complete by simply _____ the **subordinating conjunction** to form an independent clause.

Cross out the subordinating conjunction in each of the following clauses to make an independent clause:

    Because Tana is already here.

Before the house was built.

Another way to fix fragments is to combine the dependent clause with an _____ _____. The subordinating conjunction should link the clauses and _____ the relationship between them.

On Your Own

Use the suggested methods to re-write the following fragments.

1. Add the missing subject or verb.

    Once inside the house

2. Add an independent clause.

    Even though I could read the words

Run-on Sentences

A **run-on sentence** happens when:

Compound Sentences

When two independent clauses are combined, they form a _____ _____. Both halves of the sentence express a _____ thought.

Example:
    The highway was very busy today. I took the bus instead.

Compound sentences are always joined in one of three ways:

1.

2.

3.

Comma Splice

A comma splice incorrectly joins two independent clauses with only a _____.

List the four ways to fix a comma splice:

1.   3.

2.   4.

Fused Sentences

A fused sentence is another type of _____-_____ sentence. It is an incomplete sentence in which two _____ are connected without the _____ punctuation.

List the four ways to fix fused sentences:

1. 3.

2. 4.

On Your Own

Use the suggested methods to rewrite the following run-on sentences:

1. Add a semicolon.

   I leave work every day as the sun is going down the traffic is always terrible.

2. Add a conjunction.

   The freshly squeezed orange juice is very good, I drink it every morning.

3. Separate the independent clauses into two sentences.

   The socks are in the top drawer the shirts are in the closet.

4. Use a semicolon and a conjunctive adverb.

   She is not speaking to me, I would've helped her.

Lesson Wrap-up

Key Terms

Define the Key Terms from this lesson.

Comma:

Comma Splice:

Complete Sentence:

Compound Sentence:

Conjunction:

Lesson Wrap-up

Conjunctive Adverb:

Coordinating Conjunction:

Dependent Clause:

Fragment:

Fused Sentence:

Independent Clause:

Phrase:

Run-on Sentence:

Semicolon:

Subordinating Conjunction:

Lesson 4.9
Using Consistent Subjects and Verbs

OBJECTIVES

★ Recognize and apply subject-verb agreement.
★ Identify indefinite pronouns.
★ Apply subject-verb agreement with indefinite pronouns.
★ Recognize the characteristics of a sentence.

BIG IDEA

Using consistent subjects and verbs creates stability and rhythm in your writing and allows your readers to better understand your main point without the obstacle of awkward language.

In this lesson, you will learn about the following:

- Recognizing Subject-Verb Agreement
- Identifying Situations with Abnormal Subject-Verb Agreement

Recognizing Subject-Verb Agreement

All subjects and verbs are either _____ or _____.

Complete the following chart with the missing subjects and verbs.

Singular Subject	Singular Verb	Plural Subject	Plural Verb
dog	scratches	dogs	scratch
person		people	
friend	jumps		jump

Identifying Situations with Abnormal Subject-Verb Agreement

While subject-verb agreement is fairly _____, it can be tricky to achieve in sentences that have these features:

1.   4.

2.   5.

3.

Identifying Situations with Abnormal Subject-Verb Agreement   143

Compound Subjects

Define the term **compound subject**.

If the sentence uses the conjunctions _____ or _____, the subject is

_____.

Underline the compound subjects in the following sentences:

   Jamal and Sarah have turned in their homework.

   Both Aiden and Lisa have been to see me.

If the sentence uses any of the following conjunctions, the subject _____ to the verb determines the number.

1.
2.
3.
4.

Indefinite Pronouns

Define the term **indefinite pronoun**.

Grammar Practice 1

Identify the indefinite pronoun functioning as the subject of each sentence. Check your work using the Answer Key in the back of the book.

   Nothing you say will ever change my mind.

   Somebody rang my doorbell at 3:00 a.m.

To determine whether the words *all*, *any*, *most*, *none*, or *some* are plural, look at the _____

of the _____.

Collective Nouns as Subjects

Collective nouns _____ a group but are treated as _____ nouns.

Lesson 4.9 | Using Consistent Subjects and Verbs

On Your Own

For each of the following sentences, check the box next to the correct verb.

Our football team _____ going to the state playoffs.
- ☐ is
- ☐ are

The entire cast _____ offered free season tickets at the theatre.
- ☐ was
- ☐ were

Mr. Simpson's class _____ in the library on Friday mornings.
- ☐ meet
- ☐ meets

Mount Bethel's choir _____ at nursing homes every Sunday.
- ☐ sings
- ☐ sing

Distracting Words and Phrases

The more words and phrases that come between a _____ and its _____, the more confusing that sentence seems.

Example:

The herd of elephants in the wild trampled everything in its path.
The herd ~~of elephants in the wild~~ trampled everything ~~in its path~~.

Grammar Practice 2

Read the following sentences and follow the instructions provided. Check your work using the Answer Key in the back of the book.

The residents of that beautiful villa (have/has) left for the winter.

1. Cross out the two prepositional phrases in this sentence.
2. Underline the subject of this sentence.
3. Circle the appropriate verb that agrees with the subject of this sentence.

The houses in the path of the hurricane (was/were) destroyed.

1. Cross out the two prepositional phrases in this sentence.
2. Underline the subject of this sentence.
3. Circle the appropriate verb that agrees with the subject of this sentence.

Inverted Word Order

In a sentence with **regular word order**, the subject comes _____ the _____.

Sentences with **inverted word order** switch the locations of these sentence parts, so the _____ comes before the _____.

Example:

Into the pool <u>jump</u> several excited <u>children</u>.

On Your Own

Read the following paragraph and identify the sentence that does not use correct subject-verb agreement.

Photographs and video clips from the World Trade Center attacks on September 11, 2001, recall the fear and uncertainty that gripped the entire nation. Even for those who did not personally experience the loss of a loved one, images such as The Falling Man symbolizes the thousands of people killed on that day. This tragic, yet simple news photograph and others like it have accumulated more meaning and significance than the photographers could have imagined.

Lesson Wrap-up

Key Terms

Define the following terms from this lesson.

Collective Noun:

Complete Sentence:

Compound Subject:

Conjunction:

Indefinite Pronoun:

Inverted Word Order:

Number:

Phrase:

Prepositional Phrase:

Regular Word Order:

Subject:

Subject-Verb Agreement:

Verb:

Lesson 4.10
Using Consistent Pronouns and Antecedents

OBJECTIVES

★ Recognize pronouns and antecedents.
★ Recognize pronoun-antecedent agreement.
★ Apply pronoun-antecedent agreement.
★ Recognize subject-verb agreement.
★ Define pronouns.

BIG IDEA

Using pronouns makes your writing smoother and less repetitive. While pronouns are easy to use, they follow a strict set of rules. Understanding these rules will improve the clarity of your writing.

In this lesson, you will learn about the following:

- Reference & Antecedents
- Agreement

Reference & Antecedents

Pronouns *refer* to _____ or other _____. This **reference** should be clear. Pronouns must _____ with their antecedents in three ways:

1.

2.

3.

On Your Own

Read the sentences in the following table. Then, replace *they* with a specific noun.

I went to the doctor's office, but <u>they</u> told me to see a dentist.

I went to the doctor's office, but _____ told me to see a dentist.

After touring the ruins of the Roman Colosseum, <u>they</u> took a train to Florence.

After touring the ruins of the Roman Colosseum, _____ took a train to Florence.

Agreement

Gender

The gender of a pronoun must match the gender of its _____.

Agreement

Complete the following sentences with a pronoun that matches the gender of the antecedent.

Male   That man mows _____ yard every Saturday.

Female   Kayla left _____ purse on the subway.

Neutral   The maple tree is losing _____ leaves.

Number

Pronouns can also be _____ or _____. *Singular* refers to _____ thing, and *plural* refers to _____ things.

Singular antecedents are _____ paired with singular pronouns; plural antecedents are _____ paired with plural pronouns.

Define the term **indefinite pronoun**.

When a sentence contains a _____ **subject**, you must use special guidelines to decide if the subject is singular or plural.

A subject that is joined by the conjunctions _____ or _____ is plural. If the sentence uses *nor, or, neither/nor,* or *either/or,* use the subject _____ to the verb to decide if it's singular or plural.

On Your Own

Read the following paragraph and identify the sentence with a pronoun and antecedent that do not agree in gender and/or number.

> Little is known about the subjective experience of breast cancer survivors after primary treatment. However, these experiences are important because it shapes their communication about their illness in everyday life. The present study investigated this topic by combining qualitative and quantitative methods.
> (Excerpt courtesy of "Breast Cancer Survivors' Recollection of Their Illness and Therapy" by Patricia Lindberg, et al.)

Lesson Wrap-up

Key Terms

Write the number of each term next to its definition.

1. Number
2. Conjunction
3. Subject
4. Antecedent
5. Verb
6. Noun
7. Pronoun-Antecedent Agreement
8. Compound Subject
9. Gender
10. Pronoun
11. Indefinite Pronoun

_____ The word that a pronoun renames in a sentence

_____ A subject made up of two nouns or pronouns, usually joined by a conjunction

_____ A word that makes a connection between other words or a group of words

_____ A basis for classifying feminine, masculine, and neutral words

_____ A pronoun that does not rename a specific noun

_____ A word that represents a person, place, thing, event, or idea

_____ A basis for agreement between singular or plural words

_____ A word that takes the place of a noun in a sentence

_____ The consistency in gender and number between a pronoun and the person, place, thing, idea, or event it renames in a sentence

_____ The person, place, thing, event, or idea a sentence is about

_____ A word that represents an action, relationship, or state of being

Lesson 4.11
Using Correct Pronoun Reference and Case

OBJECTIVES

- ★ Identify objective, subjective, and possessive pronouns.
- ★ Identify pronoun case.
- ★ Identify pronoun reference errors.
- ★ Recognize correct pronoun case.
- ★ Recognize and understand pronoun-antecedent agreement.

BIG IDEA

To ensure that your writing is as effective as possible, pay close attention to pronoun case.

In this lesson, you will learn how to:

- Identify Subjective, Objective, and Possessive Pronoun Case
- Apply Correct Case with Difficult Wording
- Use Correct Pronoun Reference

Identify Subjective, Objective, and Possessive Pronoun Case

Personal pronouns have three main functions in a sentence:

1.

2.

3.

You must make sure that the _____ of the pronoun matches the way the pronoun is being used in the sentence.

Complete the following table of subjective, objective, and possessive pronouns.

Subjective	Objective	Possessive
I		mine
	you	
she		hers
he		
	them	their/theirs
we		
	it	

Subjective Case

Subjective-case pronouns are always used as the _____ of a sentence.

Add a subjective-case pronoun to each of the following sentences:

After the movie, _____ went out for ice cream.

Jane and _____ didn't like the movie.

Objective Case

Objective-case pronouns are used in two ways:

1.

2.

Direct objects follow a _____ and receive some kind of _____. **Indirect objects** receive the _____ _____.

Add an objective-case pronoun to each of the following sentences:

Watch _____ while the family is out of town.

The professor gave _____ the graded tests to hand out.

Possessive Case

Possessive pronouns show _____. They can function as _____ or as _____ pronouns.

Add a possessive-case pronoun to each of the following sentences:

That is _____ pencil.

My mom and dad worked together to clean _____ house.

Apply Correct Case with Difficult Wording

Relative Pronouns

Relative pronouns are used to introduce _____ **clauses**.

The cat, which dad brought home, plays all the time.

In this sentence:

- What is the subject?

- What is the dependent clause?

- What is the verb in the dependent clause?
- What is the main verb?

Who and *Whom*

Who is a _____-case pronoun, and *whom* is an _____-case pronoun. To decide which one you should use in a sentence, try substituting _____ for *who* and _____ for *whom*.

Demonstrative Pronouns

Demonstrative pronouns take the place of a _____ _____ or serve as _____ in a noun phrase. If the sentence doesn't need the clause being connected, use _____. If the clause being connected is essential for clarity, the proper pronoun is _____.

Use Correct Pronoun Reference

Every time you use a pronoun, it must refer to a clear _____, or a word that a pronoun _____.

No Clear Antecedents

One common pronoun error is using a pronoun without any _____ at all. Another pronoun commonly used without an antecedent is *it*. Whenever possible, use a _____ instead.

Multiple Antecedents

A pronoun can also become confusing when it has more than _____ possible antecedent. The best way to correct this would be to:

Antecedent Rules

Finally, the antecedent of a pronoun will always be a _____, not an _____. Using a noun instead of a pronoun may feel a bit _____ in some cases.

On Your Own

Read the following paragraph and identify the sentence that contains an incorrect pronoun reference.

> After receiving an invitation to interview for her dream job at McCollum and Associates, Brenda asked her sister for help. She suggested practicing interview questions aloud. After spending over three hours preparing, Brenda felt confident about her interview skills.

Lesson Wrap-up

Key Terms

Define the following Key Terms from this lesson.

Adjective:

Antecedent:

Apostrophe:

Demonstrative Pronoun:

Dependent Clause:

Direct Object:

Indirect Object:

Noun:

Object of the Preposition:

Objective Case:

Person:

Personal Pronoun:

Possessive Case:

Prepositional Phrase:

Pronoun:

Pronoun Case:

Pronoun Reference:

Relative Pronoun:

Subject:

Subjective Case:

Verb:

Lesson 4.12
Using Commas

OBJECTIVES

★ Understand the purposes of commas.
★ Recognize correct use of commas with adjectives.
★ Recognize correct use of commas with dependent clauses.
★ Recognize correct use of commas with extra details.
★ Recognize correct use of commas with independent clauses.
★ Recognize correct use of commas with introductory phrases.
★ Recognize correct use of commas with lists.
★ Recognize correct use of commas with transitions.
★ Recognize the correct use of commas.

BIG IDEA

Commas organize words and ideas inside a sentence, making the meaning much easier to understand.

This lesson will explain how to use commas in the following situations:

- Lists
- Compound Sentences
- Introductory Words, Phrases, and Clauses
- Extra or Unnecessary Details
- Adjectives

Lists

Whenever you are listing more than _____ items, you need to _____ each one with a comma. Some people disagree about whether you need to use a comma between the last two items in a list (called the Oxford comma) since they are already joined by a _____.

Grammar Practice 1

Assume that your instructor expects you to use the Oxford comma, and insert commas where needed in the following sentences:

I bought a tent sleeping bag air mattress and hiking boots.

To get ready for the holiday season, the grocery store manager had to order extra ham flour sugar cranberry sauce green beans and pumpkin pies.

In preparing for her trip, Laura packed shampoo conditioner deodorant her passport her pillow and a map of the city.

Lesson 4.12 | Using Commas

Compound Sentences

A **compound sentence** is made up of two _____ clauses joined together by a _____ and a _____. If you forget to add the comma, the sentence is grammatically incorrect and is considered a _____ _____.

If you have a comma but forget to add a conjunction, it is considered a _____ _____ and is also grammatically incorrect.

On Your Own

The following sentences are missing commas. Rewrite each sentence, adding commas where appropriate.

The computer died after a week; consequently he was furious he had paid so much money for it.

The sun was burning bright and hot and she needed to apply sunscreen often.

I wanted to see Stacy and go to the movies with Sarah but my mother had other ideas.

On Your Own

Read the following sentences and choose the one that uses a comma incorrectly.

The music for the road trip music has been picked, but we still need to buy snacks.

The mechanics students are learning about repairing auto brakes, and manual transmissions.

Queen Victoria had nine children, and her descendants are still part of European royalty today.

Introductory Words, Phrases, and Clauses

List the common types of introductions and write an example for each:

1.
2.
3.
4.

© HAWKES LEARNING

Extra or Unnecessary Details

Some extra information is not necessary to the _____ of a sentence.

    Jonathan, who had only slept five hours the night before, felt exhausted.

However, some information is _____ to the meaning of the sentence. Often, these necessary phrases or clauses start with the word *that*.

    I need clothes that are office-appropriate for spring.

Adjectives

Commas are used to separate similar _____ adjectives of equal weight. If you can insert the word *and* between the adjectives, you should use a _____.

Lesson Wrap-up

Test Yourself

Add commas where necessary in the sentences below. Check your work using the Answer Key in the back of the book.

1. Finally you will add the flour to the egg mixture.
2. Additionally you will need to buy your own camping gear for this trip.
3. After the train passed it took twenty minutes for us to get through the backed-up traffic.
4. By that time Annie was already gone.
5. Even though I was tired I stayed up late to finish the movie.
6. Although my sister was younger than I she was always bossing me around.
7. Excuse me you must never talk like that to your mother again.

Key Terms

Beside each definition, write the corresponding term.

_____ : A word, phrase, or sentence that shows order and makes connections between ideas

_____ : A group of related words that starts with a preposition and ends with a noun or pronoun

_____ : A word group that includes a subject and a verb and expresses a complete thought

Lesson 4.12 | Using Commas

_____: A word group that includes a subject and verb but does not express a complete thought

_____: A sentence error made when two independent clauses are improperly joined by only a comma and no conjunction

_____: A word that describes a noun or pronoun

_____: A sentence error made when two independent clauses are combined without a comma and conjunction or with only a conjunction

_____: A word that takes the place of a noun in a sentence

_____: A transition word used after a semicolon to show comparison, contrast, sequence, and other relationships

_____: A word that represents an action, relationship, or state of being

_____: Two independent clauses joined by a comma and a conjunction

_____: A word that makes a connection between other words or a group of words

_____: The person, place, thing, event, or idea a sentence is about

_____: A punctuation mark used to separate items in a list; join compound sentences; mark introductory words, phrases, and clauses; add extra or unnecessary details to a sentence; and separate similar adjectives

_____: A word or group of words that adds emphasis or emotion

_____: A word that represents a person, place, thing, event, or idea

_____: A word group that adds to the meaning of a sentence but does not express a complete thought and usually lacks a subject and a verb

Lesson 4.13
Using Semicolons and Colons

OBJECTIVES
★ Understand the purposes of colons and semicolons.
★ Understand the functions of colons and semicolons.

BIG IDEA

Because semicolons and colons are the most commonly confused punctuation marks, it is essential to learn the proper usage of both. Using colons and semicolons properly will make your writing flow smoothly.

Define the term **semicolon.**

Define the term **colon.**

In this lesson, you will learn about the following:

- Purposes and Functions of Semicolons
- Purposes and Functions of Colons

Purposes and Functions of Semicolons

If two _____ make more sense together, _____ them with a semicolon. Semicolons can also be used to separate _____ list items.

Join the following independent clauses with a semicolon.

> My company is moving to Seattle.
> They are paying me to move there.

On Your Own

Read the following sentence and identify the word that should be followed by a semicolon.

> On tour last year, the band stopped in Kansas City, Missouri, Seattle, Washington; and Sacramento, California.

Purposes and Functions of Colons

Colons can be used in four main ways:

1.
2.
3.
4.

Lists

Colons can be used after a _____ sentence to _____ a list.

When a colon is used to introduce a list, the introductory statement must be an _____ _____.

Example:

For my birthday, I want the following: a car, a hundred dollars, and a plane ticket.

Salutations

Colons can also be used in the salutation of a _____ _____. A **salutation** is the phrase that _____ the person or group receiving the letter.

Quotations

Colons can be used instead of a _____ to introduce _____. Just like lists, these quotes must follow an _____ _____.

On Your Own

Read the sentences below and identify the one that could use a colon instead of a comma.

My history professor once argued, "The only way to make progress is by paying attention to the actions of our ancestors."

My history professor once argued the following belief, "The only way to make progress is by paying attention to the actions of our ancestors."

Lesson Wrap-up

Test Yourself

Place commas, semicolons, or colons where necessary in the following sentences. Check your work using the Answer Key in the back of the book.

1. My professor made the following statement "If you come to class without your study notes, you will be asked to leave and go get them."

2. I was sick today I stayed home in bed.

3. When I was a child my dad used to like to pile the family in the car and take long drives.

4. Every time I smell a certain odor it reminds me of my grandparents' house.

5. For this art class you will need a portfolio colored pencils drawing paper and a sketching pencil.

Key Terms

Define the Key Terms from this lesson.

Colon:

Comma:

Independent Clause:

Phrase:

Salutation:

Semicolon:

Lesson 4.14
Using Apostrophes

OBJECTIVE

★ Understand the purposes of apostrophes.

BIG IDEA

Learning how to use apostrophes correctly will make you a more effective writer and help you avoid potentially embarrassing mistakes.

Define the term **apostrophe**.

In this lesson, you will learn three uses for apostrophes:
- Possessive Nouns
- Contractions
- Shortened Numbers and Words

Possessive Nouns

A possessive noun shows _____ of an item. These **nouns** _____ use an apostrophe. To make a **singular noun** possessive, add an _____ and the letter -s to words that don't already end in -s and just an apostrophe to words that do end in -s.

To make a plural noun possessive, add an _____ and the letter -s to words that don't already end in -s and _____ an apostrophe to words that do end in -s.

Complete the following table using the examples from the lesson.

Possessive Plural Nouns without -s	Possessive Plural Nouns with -s

Grammar Practice 1

Shorten the following phrases, using apostrophes to indicate possession.

the car belonging to Mark	
the house belonging to Jane	

the newspaper that was delivered yesterday	
the marriage license received by the couple	
the symptoms shared by two or more patients	

Common Mistakes

When using apostrophes, people make three common mistakes:

1.
2.
3.

On Your Own

Identify the apostrophe error in each of the following sentences:

Andrew's family and three of his best friend's are going to help him set up the tents in the backyard.

The cabin is their's, but when it's tourist season they rent it out.

Nicole's and Kalyn's apartment is within walking distance of some good restaurants.

Contractions

A **contraction** is a _____ that has been shortened into _____ _____.

Complete the following table with the correct contraction or phrase.

Phrase	Contraction
cannot	
	hasn't
he will	
	it's
let us	

Shortened Numbers and Words

The final use for apostrophes is shortening _____ and _____.

Complete the following table with the correct shortened number or phrase.

Long	Shortened
of the clock	
hanging out	
madam	
1990s	

Lesson Wrap-up

Test Yourself

Insert correct apostrophes in the following sentences. Check your work using the Answer Key in the back of the book.

Im hungry, so lets eat right now.

That car is hers, but shes not taking very good care of it.

My great-grandfather was born in the 1880s and he lived until the late 80s (1980s, that is).

I used to prefer to play at all my cousins homes instead of my own.

The childrens home that is for needy children is funded by the state.

Key Terms

Define the following Key Terms from this lesson.

Apostrophe:

Contraction:

Phrase:

Plural Noun:

Possessive Case:

Pronoun:

Singular Noun:

Lesson 4.15
Using Quotation Marks, Parentheses, and Brackets

OBJECTIVES

★ Understand the purposes of quotation marks, parentheses, and brackets.
★ Recognize the functions of quotation marks, parentheses, and brackets.

BIG IDEA

Sometimes, sentences contain words that are nonessential to the meaning of the text or are quoted from another source.

In this lesson, you will learn about the purposes of the following punctuation marks:

- Quotation Marks
- Parentheses
- Brackets

Quotation Marks

Quotation marks are most commonly used to _____ someone else's _____. They are often used around certain types of titles, including:

1.   4.

2.   5.

3.

On Your Own

Read the sentence below and identify the word that should be followed by quotation marks.

"You need to start reading more, Grandma proclaimed.

Periods, commas, exclamation points, and question marks that appear at the end of a quote should be placed _____ the closing quotation mark.

Parentheses

Parentheses are always used in pairs. They are used to add extra information—like _____, _____, or _____—to a sentence.

Define the term **parenthetical information**.

Lesson 4.15 | Using Quotation Marks, Parentheses, and Brackets

Parentheses are also used to introduce _____, which are shortened forms of a _____ or _____.

On Your Own

Read the following sentences and identify the one that correctly uses parentheses.

The best pet I ever had (and still have) is my dog Leroy. He's a little guy who only weighs twelve pounds, but he's (very friendly and excitable.)

Brackets

Brackets are most commonly used _____ parentheses or quotation marks to add _____ details or _____. Brackets can also be used to insert _____ _____ inside a quotation.

On Your Own

Read the sentences below and select the one that correctly uses brackets.

All local universities are involved with the experiment (other than University of North Carolina [UNC]). They've decided to remain uninvolved as they don't agree with [the morality] of the research procedure.

Lesson Wrap-up

Key Terms

Write the number of each term next to its definition.

1. Parentheses
2. Brackets
3. Quotation Marks
4. Abbreviation
5. Single Quotation Marks
6. Parenthetical Information

_____ A shortened form of a word or phrase

_____ A pair of punctuation marks commonly used inside parentheses or quotation marks to add minor details to a sentence or insert missing text inside a quotation

_____ A pair of punctuation marks used to add extra information to a sentence or introduce an abbreviation

_____ In-text details that are set off by parentheses and provide extra information

_____ A pair of punctuation marks most commonly used to repeat someone else's words

_____ Punctuation marks used to mark a quote or title within a quote

Lesson 4.16
Using Ellipses, Hyphens, and Dashes

OBJECTIVES

- ★ Understand the purposes of ellipses, hyphens, and dashes.
- ★ Recognize the functions of ellipses, hyphens, and dashes.
- ★ Learn to properly use ellipses, hyphens, and dashes.

BIG IDEA

Ellipses, hyphens, and dashes play an important role in connecting and emphasizing the ideas in your writing.

In this lesson, you will learn about how to correctly use the following punctuation marks:

- Ellipses
- Hyphens
- Dashes

Ellipses

An ellipsis is made up of three _____ in a row. Their purpose is to show that information has been _____ from a quotation.

Always add spaces _____ and _____ an ellipsis, as well as between each of the _____.

On Your Own

Read the following passage and identify the sentence that correctly uses an ellipsis.

"There are some people who believe that controversial books should be banned, … without exception, from our high schools. Some folks find certain content in this literature to … unacceptable. [John Stoe] supports my decision to stand against these individuals … and do what is right by our children."

Hyphens

Hyphens are short lines that link together two _____ or _____ _____.

List the four areas in which hyphens are most commonly used:

1.
2.

3.

4.

Compound Nouns

Compound nouns are **nouns** made up of _____ or more words. Sometimes, these words are _____ _____ with hyphens.

Compound Adjectives

Compound adjectives are two or more words that are being used to describe a _____ or _____.

To make a true compound adjective, _____ of the words must be _____ to the meaning of the sentence.

Prefixes

Prefixes are word parts added to the _____ of a word in order to create a new word.

Numbers

Finally, hyphens can be used to spell out _____ and _____ between _____-_____ and _____-_____.

On Your Own

Identify which of the following words use hyphens correctly.

   Ex-con
   Fifty-three
   Happy-friendly
   Anti-makeup

Dashes

A **dash** is a line slightly longer than a hyphen. Dashes are sometimes called "_____-_____" because they are around the same _____ as a lowercase letter *m*.

Never add _____ before or after a dash.

Dashes should be used when the information being added to the sentence already _____ a number of _____. Dashes are also used to give greater _____ to extra_____.

On Your Own

Read the following passage and identify the sentence that correctly uses dashes.

> My mom—who raised eight children—was still able to work her entire life. She poured her blood – sweat—and tears into that job in order to support us kids.

Lesson Wrap-up

Key Terms

Define the following Key Terms from this lesson.

Adjective:

Brackets:

Comma:

Compound Adjective:

Compound Noun:

Dash:

Ellipsis:

Fragment:

Hyphen:

Noun:

Prefix:

Parentheses:

Lesson 4.17
Using Capitalization and Italics

OBJECTIVES

★ Understand capitalization rules.
★ Understand the purposes of capitalization and italics.

BIG IDEA

Capitalization and italics are both used in writing as visual markers to set apart words and phrases. They should be used sparingly, but these helpful tools remind your audience to pay close attention, as important or unique information is to come.

In this lesson, you will learn about how to correctly use the following:

- Capitalization
- Italics

Capitalization

Write the six most common uses of capital letters:

1.
2.
3.
4.
5.
6.

Sentences

You should always capitalize the _____ _____ in any sentence. If you are using an **inline quotation**, you do not need to use a capital letter at the beginning.

Proper Nouns

Capitalize **proper nouns**, which are words that name a specific _____, _____, _____, _____, or _____.

On Your Own

Read the examples and then fill in your own.

Proper Nouns	Examples	Add Your Own
People	George Takei Una Thompson	

Places	Mount Kilimanjaro Brazil	
Organizations	Kraft Foods Harvard University	
Days, months, and holidays	Monday Yom Kippur	
Historical events and eras	the Civil War Prohibition	
Ethnicities and nationalities	Asian American Cherokee	
Religions and deities	Hinduism Christianity	
Titles	"The Raven" *The Scarlet Letter*	

Other Uses

Capitalization should also be used in the following situations:

Italics

Italics are _____ letters that are used to _____ _____ certain words or phrases.

Italics are generally used for:

What are the seven types of longer works that should be italicized?

On Your Own

Fill in the table below with original sentences that use important words and foreign terms.

Important Words	Foreign Terms

Lesson Wrap-up

Key Terms

Match the lesson's Key Terms with their definitions.

a) Italics
b) Proper Noun
c) Article
d) Inline Quotation
e) Preposition
f) Coordinating Conjunction
g) Phrase

_____ An adjective (a, an, or the) that indicates whether a noun is specific or general

_____ Slanted letters most often used to set apart titles of longer works, important words, and foreign terms

_____ A word group that adds to the meaning of a sentence but does not express a complete thought and usually lacks a subject and a verb

_____ A capitalized noun that represents a specific person, place, thing, event, or idea

_____ A conjunction that connects words or word groups of equal importance in a sentence

_____ A quote that fits into a sentence without a formal introduction

_____ A word that shows a relationship among people, places, things, and ideas

Lesson 4.18
Using Abbreviations and Numbers

OBJECTIVES
- ★ Understand abbreviation rules.
- ★ Understand the spelling rules for numbers.

BIG IDEA

Different types of abbreviations and numbers follow their own sets of rules.

In this lesson, you will learn how to correctly use the following:
- Abbreviations
- Numbers

Abbreviations

Abbreviations are:

On Your Own

Add some more examples to the following table.

Types	Examples	Add Your Own
Organizations	WHO (World Health Organization) WWE (World Wrestling Entertainment) CDC (Center for Disease Control)	
Titles	Mr. Myerson Ms. Bennet Dr. Spaulding	
Initials	J. K. Rowling O. J. Simpson Susan B. Anthony	
Units	6 lbs. 56 ft. 4 tsp.	
Dates and Times	Jan. 6:00 p.m. 2459 BCE	

States	MN	
	SC	
	PA	

When using the _____ of an organization in a piece of writing, use the full name first, followed by the _____ in _____. Afterwards, you only need to use the abbreviation.

Numbers

In math class, you will almost always use _____, like 9 or 67, when you are talking about numbers. In an English paper, however, you would _____ those same numbers out as _____ or _____-_____. You should also use words to _____ a larger number (like $3.5 million.)

When should you use actual numbers, or numerals?

On Your Own

Read the paragraph below and identify a sentence that uses numbers correctly.

> The 4 company headquarters owned by Liberty, Inc. house a wide variety of careers and professional opportunities. There are a total of twenty thousand employees and ninety-five management positions. Each headquarters contains roughly twenty-five departments. Their customer base is large as well; they serve a population of 1,500,000 clients.

Lesson Wrap-up

Key Terms

Define the Key Terms from this lesson.

Abbreviation:

Hyphen:

Parentheses:

Phrase:

Lesson 4.19
Using Basic Spelling Rules

OBJECTIVES

- ★ Understand basic spelling rules.
- ★ Understand how to spell *ie* and *ei* words.
- ★ Understand how to spell plural words.
- ★ Understand how to spell words with final consonants.
- ★ Understand how to spell words with suffixes.

BIG IDEA

Correct spelling is crucial in academic and professional settings if you want to make a good impression.

In this lesson, you will learn useful spelling rules for the following situations:

- *IE* and *EI* Words
- Plural Words
- Suffixes

IE and *EI* Words

One old spelling rule that people often remember is:

Fill in the table with examples from the lesson.

ie	After *c*	Words like *weigh*

Exceptions

Use *ie* after the *-sh* sound:

Use *ei* if the vowels are pronounced like the *i* in *bit*:

Use *ei* in abnormal words:

On Your Own

Choose the correctly spelled word. Rewrite the others with the correct spelling of each.

- ☐ Reciept
- ☐ Ancient
- ☐ Foriegn
- ☐ Releif

Plural Words

When you are making a word plural, pay attention to the _____ of the word. Add -es to any words that end with the following letters:

If a word ends in any other letter, follow this rule:

On Your Own

Read the table of plural words below and fill in the blanks with your own examples.

-es	-s
mess → messes	assignment → assignments
brush → brushes	caterpillar → caterpillars
church → churches	nap → naps
box → boxes	phone → phones
peach → peaches	scissor → scissors

Words that end in _____ are a special exception to this rule. Some are spelled with -es and some are spelled with -s. If you aren't sure which one to use, be sure to check a dictionary.

On Your Own

Read the table of plural words that end in -o below and fill in the blanks with your own examples.

-es	-s
echo → echoes	combo → combos
hero → brushes	logo → logos

potato → potatoes	taco → tacos
tomato → tomatoes	typo → typos
veto → vetoes	video → videos

Finally, remember that some words _____ their spelling or _____ _____ _____ when they are made plural.

On Your Own

Read the tables below and fill in the blanks with your own examples.

Singular	Plural (Spelling Changes)
child	children
goose	geese
mouse	mice
person	people

Singular	Plural (Spelling Stays the Same)
deer	deer
fish	fish
sheep	sheep
species	species

Suffixes

Suffixes are _____ _____ added to the end of a root in order to change the meaning.

Silent -e

Many words in the English language end in a silent -e. If you are adding a suffix that starts with a vowel to the word, drop the silent -e.

On Your Own

Read the table below and fill in the blanks with your own examples.

Original	Vowel Suffix	Loses e
Dance	-ing	Dancing
Narrate	-ion	Narration
Excite	-able	Excitable
File	-ed	filed

On Your Own

Read the table below and fill in the blanks with your own examples.

Original	Vowel Suffix	Loses e
advertise	-ment	advertisement
hope	-ful	hopeful
safe	-ty	safety
state	-ly	stately

Final -y

When the letter before the final -y is a vowel, follow this rule:

On Your Own

Read the table below and fill in the blanks with your own examples for different final -y scenarios.

Original	Suffix	New
employ	-er	employer
enjoy	-ing	enjoying
try	-s	tries
mystery	-ous	mysterious

Final Consonants

When adding a _____ to a one-syllable word that ends with a *consonant-vowel-consonant* pattern, you must _____ the final consonant. (A **syllable** is a basic unit of a word's pronunciation.)

Examples:
   jam → jamming
   snap → snapped

On Your Own

Read the table below and fill in the blanks with your own examples for different final consonant scenarios.

Original	New
sit	sitting
knot	knotting
refer	referred
submit	submitting

Lesson Wrap-up

Key Terms

Define the Key Terms from this lesson.

Stress:

Suffix:

Syllable:

Lesson 4.20
Spelling Commonly Confused Words

OBJECTIVES
- ★ Learn how to spell commonly confused words.
- ★ Learn how to spell commonly misspelled words.

BIG IDEA

Learning the definitions and functions of confusing words will help you utilize them properly.

This lesson will teach you the differences between two types of commonly misused words:
- Similar Sound Words
- Similar Meaning Words

Similar Sound Words

Write a brief definition or description that will help you remember the meaning of each word:

Accept:	Except:	Affect:	Effect:
Its:	It's:	Loose:	Lose:
Choose:	Chose:	Its:	It's:
Past:	Passed:	Than:	Then:
There:	Their:	They're:	Too:

© HAWKES LEARNING

Lesson 4.20 | Spelling Commonly Confused Words

To:	Two:	Whether:	Weather:
Whose:	Who's:	Your:	You're

Similar Meaning Words

Words with similar meanings are called _____. Words with opposite meanings are called _____.

Write a brief definition or description that will help you remember the meaning of each word:

Between:	Among:
Borrow:	Lend:
Come:	Go:
Fewer:	Less:
Lie:	Lay:

On Your Own

Read the following sentences and determine which word fits in the blank.

Let's meet at (your / you're) place to work on the group project.

The squirrel stopped in (its / it's) tracks in the middle of the sidewalk.

When it's hot outside, wear (loose / lose) clothing and drink water regularly.

My friend (lends / borrows) pens from me in class and never gives them back.

The article claimed that (less / fewer) music has been illegally downloaded this year.

Every day at three o'clock, my grandfather (lays / lies) down to take a nap.

Test Yourself

Identify the correct word in the sentences below. Check your work using the Answer Key in the back of the book.

1. Do not (accept / except) friend requests from people you don't know.
2. How did that medicine (effect / affect) you?
3. The mouse hid (its / it's) cheese in the hole in the wall.
4. I love studying about our nation's (past / passed).
5. I could not get the knots in my shoelaces (loose / lose).
6. Which kind of cheesecake did you (choose / chose)?
7. I'd rather go swimming (than / then) do my chores.
8. Her house is over (there / their).
9. (Their / They're) moving into a new home.
10. Would you like to come with us, (to / too)?
11. We are going (to / too) the movies.
12. Oh, the (whether / weather) outside is frightful.
13. Have you found out (whose / who's) keys those are?
14. (Your / You're) going to get into trouble if you don't stop it.
15. Just (between / among) you and me, I hated that cake.
16. Will you please (come / go) over here and help me.
17. There are (fewer / less) students in my class this semester.
18. I have a headache, so I will (lay / lie) here for a while.

Lesson Wrap-up

Key Terms

Define the Key Terms from this lesson.

Adjective:

Antonym:

Adverb:

Contraction:

Homonym:

Noun:

Preposition:

Pronoun:

Subordinating Conjunction:

Synonym:

Verb:

Lesson 4.21
Proofreading Sentences for Grammar

OBJECTIVES

★ Learn a process for proofreading for grammar.
★ Proofread for grammar errors involving punctuation.

BIG IDEA

Being able to correct your own writing errors will help you present yourself and your ideas in a more professional and academic way.

In this lesson, you will learn about the following strategies:

- Make a List of Your Common Mistakes
- Proofread in Stages
- Try Multiple Reading Techniques
- Take Advantage of Technology
- Take Frequent Breaks

Make a List of Your Common Mistakes

List five of your most common grammar/spelling mistakes:

1. 4.

2. 5.

3

Proofread in Stages

Trying to catch all of your grammar and spelling errors in just one reading is _____.

To make the best use of your time, start with your most _____ grammar and spelling mistakes.

Proofreading Checklist: Grammatical Sentences

✓ Sentence Structure:

✓ Agreement:

✓ Punctuation:

✓ Spelling:

Try Multiple Reading Techniques

Name two reading strategies that are better than reading silently when you proofread:

1.   2.

On Your Own

Apply the above reading strategies as you proofread the following passage. Write down your corrections.

> So, why don't we, as a society, continue to volunteer past adolescence and into adulthood. Many argue that lack of time is the biggest factor preventing college students and young workers from giving to others. However, when a person gives of his time. He learns to see the world through the eyes of those who benefit from his volunteering. For example, a woman who helps distribute food at a food pantry sees the need in her community. She sees the value of sacrificcing a couple of hours a month; to give to others who may need some temporary help in order to survive. Because she can put a face to that need, they are willing to give up some of her down time. the activities that used to take up her off-work hours, such as television, become less engaging than the satisfaction of improving another's life.

Take Advantage of Technology

List two ways you can take advantage of technology while you proofread:

On Your Own

Read the sentence below and identify the misspelled word.

> Gaming is now headed into the new teritory of virtual reality.

Take Frequent Breaks

_____ to _____ minutes should be plenty of time for you to stretch your legs or get a drink.

Don't allow yourself to take too much time, however, as you might become _____.

Lesson Wrap-up

On Your Own

Read the following excerpt from a student essay on the brain's role in processing depression. Identify grammatical errors and make corrections.

Many self-help gurus turn to notions of self-empowerment and willfulness to encourage depressed individuals to engage the world. However, this sort of instruction ignore what many current scientists and philosophers know: a person's ability to control his or her own thoughts is extremely limited. In his essay, Jack Burton explains that "lower-level brain modules can profoundly affect not only our ordinary sensory perceptions but also how we experience abstract symbols" (65). He goes on to explain that these lower-level processes actually precede feelings of certainty when people make decisions, so unconscious thinking actually underwrites human actions Thus, it is not at all clear that positive thinking is within a person's control. While many people don't believe this to be true.

Chapter 4 Key Terms

The following Key Terms bank includes grammar topics covered throughout this chapter. Refer to this list for grammar help.

Action Verb	a verb that indicates a physical or mental action
Adjective	a word that describe a noun or a pronoun
Adverb	a part of speech that describes a verb, adjective, or another adverb
Antecedent	the word that a pronoun renames in a sentence
Antonym	a word that has the opposite meaning of another word
Apostrophe	a punctuation mark used for possessive nouns, contractions, and shortened numbers and words
Base Form	the simplest form of a verb, free of alterations for tense, number, and point of view
Brackets	a pair of punctuation marks commonly used inside parentheses or quotation marks to add minor details to a sentence or insert missing text inside a quotation
Clause	a word group that contains a subject and a verb
Colon	a punctuation mark used to introduce a list or quotation, end a salutation, and join related numbers
Comma Splice	a sentence error made when two independent clauses are improperly joined by only a comma and no conjunction

Comma	a punctuation mark used to separate items in a list; join compound sentences; mark introductory words, phrases, and clauses; add extra or unnecessary details to a sentence; and separate similar adjectives
Common Noun	a noun that represents a non-specific person, place, thing, event, or idea
Complete Sentence	a sentence that contains at least one subject and one predicate and expresses a complete thought
Complete Thought	when a group of words is logically finished
Complex Sentence	a sentence pattern in which an independent clause is connected to a dependent clause
Compound Noun	a noun made up of two or more words
Compound Sentence	a sentence pattern in which two independent clauses are connected by a comma and a coordinating conjunction
Compound Subject	a subject made up of two nouns or pronouns, usually joined by a conjunction
Compound-Complex Sentence	a sentence pattern containing at least two independent clauses and at least one dependent clause
Conjunction	a part of speech that connects two or more words, phrases, or clauses in a sentence
Conjunctive Adverb	a transition word that shows contrast, comparison, sequence, and other relationships between clauses
Contraction	a phrase that has been shortened into one word
Coordinating Conjunction	a conjunction that connects words or word groups of equal importance in a sentence
Correlative Conjunctions	conjunctions that connect two or more similar ideas and always appear in pairs
Count Noun	a noun that can be counted
Declarative Sentence	a sentence that makes a general statement that informs the reader
Demonstrative Pronoun	a pronoun that takes the place of a noun phrase and acts as an adjective
Dependent Clause	a word group that contains a subject and a verb but does not express a complete thought

Direct Object	a word that receives the action of a verb
Direct Question	a sentence that asks the audience a question and usually ends with a question mark
Exclamation Point	a punctuation mark that conveys emphasis or strong feeling
Exclamatory Sentence	a sentence that communicates emotion or surprise
FANBOYS	an acronym for the seven coordinating conjunctions
First-Person Pronoun	a pronoun used to refer to the speaker of the sentence
Fused Sentence	a sentence error made when two independent clauses are combined without a comma and conjunction or with only a conjunction
Future Tense	a verb tense used to describe an action that has not yet taken place or to describe plans or instructions
Future-Perfect Tense	a verb tense used to describe an action that started in the past and will be completed in the future
Future-Progressive Tense	a verb tense used to describe a continuous action that will take place in the future
Gender	a basis for classifying feminine, masculine, and neutral words
Gerund	a verbal that functions as a noun in a sentence and is formed by adding *–ing* to the end of the verb
Helping Verb	a verb that is added to a main verb to create a new verb that grammatically fits the sentence
Homonym	a word whose pronunciation sounds similar to that of another word
Hyphen	a short line that links together two words or word parts
Imperative Sentence	a sentence that makes commands and often addresses the implied subject
Implied Subject	the subject of a sentence when the speaker is talking directly to the audience
Indefinite Pronoun	a pronoun that does not rename a specific noun
Independent Clause	a group of words with a subject and a verb that expresses a complete thought

Indirect Object	a word that receives the direct object of a sentence
Indirect Question	a sentence that tells the audience about a question and usually ends with a period
Infinitive	a verbal that can function as a noun, adjective, or adverb in a sentence
Interjection	a word or group of words that adds emphasis or emotion
Interrogative Sentence	a sentence that asks a question
Linking Verb	a verb that connects the subject to a description
Main Verb	the verb that expresses the primary action or state of being of a subject in a complete sentence
Non-count Noun	a noun that cannot be counted
Noun	a part of speech that represents a person, place, thing, event, or idea
Number	a basis for agreement between singular or plural words
Object of the Preposition	a word that completes the meaning of a prepositional phrase
Objective Case	the form a word takes when used as the object of a preposition, direct object, or indirect object of a sentence
Objective Pronoun	a pronoun that functions as an object in a sentence
Participle Phrase	a phrase that uses a present or a past participle to introduce the rest of the sentence
Parts of Speech	the categories that classify each type of word found in a sentence
Past Participle	a verb form that can function as an adjective or as part of a perfect-tense verb to show completed mental or physical action
Past Tense	a verb tense used to report on an event or reflect on a past experience
Past-Perfect Tense	a verb tense used to describe an action that was completed before another past-completed action
Past-Progressive Tense	a verb tense used to describe a continuous action that occurred at a certain time in the past

Period	a punctuation mark used to end sentences that make a statement or relay information
Person	the point of view—first-, second-, or third-person—indicated by the form a word takes on in a sentence
Personal Pronoun	a pronoun that renames a specific person, animal, object, or place
Plural Noun	a noun that represents multiple people, places, things, events, or ideas
Possessive Case	a pronoun form that shows possession or functions as an adjective
Possessive Pronoun	a pronoun that shows possession of another noun
Predicate	the part of a sentence that indicates what a subject says or does and includes a main verb + any corresponding helping verbs
Preposition	a word that shows a relationship among people, places, things, events, and ideas
Prepositional Phrase	a group of related words that starts with a preposition and ends with a noun or pronoun
Present Participle	a verb form that can function as an adjective as part of a progressive-tense verb to express a continuous action
Present Tense	a verb tense used to describe an event or action that is happening now
Present-Perfect Tense	a verb tense used to describe an action that was started in the past and has not yet been completed
Present-Progressive Tense	a verb tense used to describe a continuous action that is happening in the present or will happen in the near future
Pronoun Case	the form a pronoun takes based on its function—subjective, objective, or possessive—in a sentence
Pronoun Reference	the connection between a pronoun and the noun it renames
Pronoun	a word that takes the place of a noun in a sentence
Pronoun-Antecedent Agreement	the consistency in gender and number between a pronoun and the person, place, thing, idea, or event it renames in a sentence
Proper Noun	a capitalized noun that represents a specific person, place, thing, event, or idea

Question Mark	a punctuation mark used at the end of a sentence that asks a question
Quotation Marks	a pair of punctuation marks used to repeat someone else's words
Relative Pronoun	a pronoun used to introduce a dependent clause
Run-on Sentence	a sentence error in which two or more independent clauses are combined improperly to create a comma splice or a fused sentence
Semicolon	a punctuation mark used to combine two independent clauses and separate items in long lists
Sentence Patterns	a set of distinct clause combinations that can make up a sentence
Simple Sentence	a sentence made up of one independent clause
Singular Noun	a noun that represents one person, place, thing, event, or idea
Subject Pronoun	a pronoun used as the subject of a sentence
Subject	the person, place, thing, event, or idea a sentence is about
Subjective Case	the form a word takes when it functions as the subject of a sentence
Subjective Pronoun	the form of a pronoun that functions as the subject in a sentence
Subject-Verb Agreement	when a subject and verb used in a sentence match in number and point of view
Subordinating Conjunction	a conjunction that introduces a dependent clause
Synonym	a word whose meaning is similar to that of another word
Verb	a word that represents an action, relationship, or state of being
Verbal	verb forms that function as other parts of speech (adjectives, adverbs, nouns) in a sentence

Chapter 5
Style

Lesson 5.1
Determining a Writing Style

OBJECTIVES

- ★ Identify strategies for determining writing style.
- ★ Identify strategies for eliminating awkwardness in writing.
- ★ Identify the formality of different genres.

BIG IDEA

As a writer, you must learn to adapt to your purpose or writing assignment while still being true to your own unique voice.

This lesson will discuss three factors that will help you determine style:

- Purpose and Audience
- Formality
- Complexity

Purpose and Audience

Describe each of the following **purposes**, or goals, for writing:

to inform:	to persuade:
to reflect:	to entertain:

Once you've decided on your purpose for writing, consider your _____: the people who will read your writing.

The _____, or attitude you express in your writing, should be appropriate for both your

_____ and your _____.

Lesson 5.1 | Determining a Writing Style

On Your Own

Imagine that you have been asked to write to a nursing class at the local college about vegetables. Identify the sentence below that would be a better addition to your paper:

☐ Vegetables are a yummy source of protein, which gives you super strong muscles.

☐ Vegetables can be a good source of protein, a nutrient that promotes muscle health.

Formality

Define the term **formality**.

Define the term **genres**.

Informal Writing

Informal writing usually uses _____-_____ and _____-_____ **pronouns** such as *I*, *me*, and *you*.

You use informal writing in your _____ _____.

Formal Writing

Formal writing is required for many _____ or _____ genres. In these situations, you use more _____ sentence structures and _____ terms and rarely use personal pronouns like *I* and *you*.

Formal writing also follows the _____ and _____ of Standard English. All of the text should be free of _____, _____, and _____ errors.

List the types of language that should be avoided in formal writing:

Complexity

Complexity doesn't have to mean "_____." **Complexity** just means that your writing has many _____ _____.

List the three questions to ask yourself before using a complex word:

1.
2.
3.

Overly-complex sentences can make a text _____ or _____ for your reader to follow. Complicated sentences can be caused by any of the following factors:

4.
5.
6.

Lesson Wrap-up

Test Yourself

Next to each text category, write **F** for Formal or **I** for Informal. Check your work using the Answer Key in the back of the book.

1. _____ Research paper
2. _____ Business proposal
3. _____ Chapter on proper nursing procedures
4. _____ Blog post about the new Italian restaurant in town
5. _____ Cover letter to a company you would like to work for
6. _____ Short story about your trip to Egypt
7. _____ Review of a book on Amazon
8. _____ Scholarly report on reading strategies

Key Terms

Beside each definition, write the corresponding term.

_____ : The positive, negative, or neutral attitude that an author expresses about a topic

_____ : The person, place, thing, event, or idea a sentence is about

_____ : A text that shares a personal experience or belief

Lesson 5.1 | Determining a Writing Style

_____: A word that takes the place of a noun in a sentence

_____: A word that shows a relationship among people, places, things, events, and ideas

_____: When a sentence is written so that the subject is receiving an action

_____: A text that gives the audience information about a topic

_____: A type of writing

_____: A text that explores a topic or event in a creative or humorous way

_____: A phrase that has been shortened into one word

_____: A popular phrase that has been overused

_____: When a sentence is written so that the subject is performing an action

_____: A word that represents an action, relationship, or state of being

_____: Abbreviations, emoticons, and other phrases used in text messages or social media

_____: Casual words or expressions specific to a particular group of people

_____: The goal of a text

_____: A group of related words that starts with a preposition and ends with a noun or pronoun

_____: A text that convinces its audience to adopt a belief or take an action

_____: The statement or argument that an author tries to communicate

_____: A phrase—unique to a certain language—that has become a cliché

_____: The way a text conforms to certain standards

_____: A word group that contains a subject and a verb but does not express a complete thought

_____: When a text has many connected parts

_____: The people who read your writing

Lesson 5.2
Using an Appropriate Tone

OBJECTIVE

★ Understand the purpose of tone in writing.

BIG IDEA

You can't use gestures or facial expressions when you write, but you can use tone. Using tone effectively will communicate your points more clearly to your readers.

Define the term **tone**.

This lesson will discuss three ways to communicate tone in your writing:
- Word Choice
- Details
- Inconsistent Tone

Word Choice

All words have _____, _____, or _____ feelings attached to them.

As you write, you must carefully select the words that will accurately reflect the _____ you want to communicate.

On Your Own

Read the following paragraphs and identify which one seems more reliable.

> *Looking Backward* is a misogynistic book that fails to represent women. The only time the author even discusses women's roles in modern society occurs during one minuscule chapter. Before this, no one knows anything about Edith other than her looks. Typically, the ladies are pushed out, leaving the big, strong men to discuss important matters by themselves (79, 128). Conditions for the women in Bellamy's vision of the year 2000 are just as bad as in 1887.

> *Looking Backward* represents women unfairly by failing to represent them at all. The only full examination of women's roles in modern society occurs during one short chapter. Before this, little is known about Edith beyond her physical beauty. Just as in the nineteenth century, the ladies retire early, leaving the men to discuss important matters by themselves (79, 128). Conditions for the women in Bellamy's vision of the year 2000 remain almost unchanged from those of 1887.

Lesson 5.2 | Using an Appropriate Tone

On Your Own

Read the following paragraph and identify the sentence that does not use the most appropriate tone.

> The leadership meeting tomorrow is mandatory. Many of the company's executives will be in attendance, so please be prompt. Also, ensure you have your laptops and up-to-date weekly reports when you arrive. The really early meeting tomorrow in the AM will be an awesome chance for us to chat about the looming lay-offs. Thank you in advance for keeping your schedule flexible.

Details

The second way to convey tone is through the details that you choose to _____ in or _____ from your writing.

If you include mainly _____ details about a topic, the tone of your writing will be more negative. If you include mainly _____ details, the tone of your writing will be more positive.

Inconsistent Tone

Writing that is _____ in tone can come across as _____.

Checklist: Tone Consistency

- ✓ _____
- ✓ _____
- ✓ _____
- ✓ _____

On Your Own

Read the following paragraph and use the previous checklist to identify the sentence with an inconsistent tone.

> Student teaching was a positive and rewarding experience. The students I taught were able to teach me so much more than I could teach them. Being in such a supportive school with hands-on parents made the semester move quickly. My principal critiqued me every single time she came into my room, which forced me to learn how to ignore negative leaders and press on. Student teaching showed me that I can imagine myself in no other profession, and I will be happy to one day have a classroom of my own.

Lesson Wrap-up

Test Yourself

Determine the tone of each word and write the corresponding letter beside it. Check your work using the Answer Key in the back of the book.

1. _____ standard   A. Negative
2. _____ elated   B. Neutral
3. _____ satisfied   C. Positive
4. _____ aggressive
5. _____ tired
6. _____ exhausted
7. _____ work
8. _____ labored
9. _____ giddy
10. _____ infuriated
11. _____ overjoyed
12. _____ unexpected
13. _____ represents

Key Terms

Define the following Key Terms from this lesson.

Audience:

Credibility:

Informative Text:

Purpose:

Tone:

Lesson 5.3
Maintaining Consistency in Tense and Person

OBJECTIVES

★ Identify shifts in tense and point of view.
★ Apply consistent tense and point of view.

BIG IDEA

Using a consistent writing style will ensure that your main idea is as clear as possible.

This lesson will help you avoid two types of inconsistencies in your writing:

- Tense
- Person

How can shifts in tense make a piece of writing confusing?

Tense

Complete the sentences below with the correct tense of each verb:

	eat	concentrate
Past	Yesterday, I _____ my favorite homecooked meal.	Sarah _____ on the goal at hand until she finally achieved success.
Present	My kitten _____ three meals per day.	The witnesses _____ on key information as they review the events of the day.
Future	At what time _____ you _____ lunch tomorrow?	I _____ _____ on that when I get a chance.

Past, Present, and Future Tense

Name two reasons why a writer might use the **present tense**:

The **past tense** is used to _____ on an event or _____ on a past experience. Many _____ books are written in the past tense.

Future Tense

The future tense is used to describe _____ or _____.

Regardless of the tense you use, be as _____ as possible. You don't want to confuse your readers by switching back and forth between tenses too frequently.

Appropriate Tense Shifts

Sometimes, a shift in tense is appropriate within a sentence or a paragraph:

On Your Own

Read the following passage and identify the paragraph that contains a shift in tense.

> Ralph tries to fill the role of authority figure by maintaining the signal fire and building shelters. He also assigns tasks to different groups of boys to ensure that they live in a civilized fashion. Unfortunately, since Ralph is only a young boy, his authority is not respected as much as an adult's authority would be respected.
>
> Piggy plays the role of the father figure, which is reflected in his appearance. He wears thick glasses, and his hair does not seem to grow. He also provides the voice of reason on the island. When the "littluns" got scared and started talking about the beast, Piggy tried to calm their fears. He maintains order by explaining that life is based on science. When Jack gets the rest of the boys frenzied about hunting, Piggy exhibits common sense by refusing to participate.

Person

It's important to maintain consistency in **person**, or point of view. There are three points of view:

1.   2.   3.

On Your Own

Read the sentences below and identify the one with a third-person point of view.

> You will want to begin the assignment by closely reading the article.
>
> We were able to determine that our mistake took place during phase one.
>
> The inmates were accused of starting the fire while the guards denied all involvement.

Personal pronouns can be categorized into first-, second-, and third-person forms. All _____ are considered third-person.

Complete the table below by filling in the singular and plural pronouns for each point of view.

Point of View	Singular	Plural
1st Person		
2nd Person		
3rd Person		

On Your Own

Read the following passage and identify the first-person pronouns.

On the last day of my sophomore year in college, my parents told me that we were going to take a family road trip that would start the next morning. When they told me, they had already packed their suitcases and mapped out the route. I dumped the contents of my dorm room into a bag, and we piled into the car. It was the beginning of a terrible summer.

In what kinds of writing is each point of view most common?

First Person: **Second Person:**   **Third Person:**

On Your Own

Rewrite each sentence so it uses a new point of view:

Do you believe pets should be allowed in restaurants?

The biker sped past us so quickly that we dropped our bags.

It's important to check over your data before submitting your lab report.

On Your Own

Read each sentence and identify its point of view.

If you want a promotion, you will have to earn it.
- ☐ First person
- ☐ Second person
- ☐ Third person

If an employee wants a promotion, he or she will have to earn it.
- ☐ First person
- ☐ Second person
- ☐ Third person

If I want a promotion, I will have to earn it.
- ☐ First person
- ☐ Second person
- ☐ Third person

On Your Own

Read the following paragraph and identify the sentence that is inconsistent in person.

Resilience is a trait that every successful person must have. Those who become successful at something often have to first fail a number of times before they reach their goal. Taylor Swift was bullied in middle school, and Katy Perry was dropped by three record labels. Both women had to overcome obstacles before achieving their goals. There have been many times I have had to pick myself up and dust myself off while trying to reach my goals. Being resilient allows a person to make mistakes, learn from them, and eventually reach his or her goal through hard work and persistence.

Lesson Wrap-up

Key Terms

Write the number of each term next to its definition.

1. Future Tense
2. Noun
3. Past Tense
4. Person
5. Personal Pronoun
6. Present Tense
7. Pronoun
8. Subject
9. Tense
10. Verb

_____ How a verb indicates when it took place: past, present, or future

_____ A word that takes the place of a noun in a sentence

_____ A pronoun that renames a specific person, animal, object, or place

_____ A verb tense used to report a past event or reflect on a past experience

_____ A verb tense used to describe an action that has not yet taken place or to describe plans or instructions

_____ A word that represents an action, relationship, or state of being

_____ The person, place, thing, event, or idea a sentence is about

_____ A verb tense used to describe an event or action that is happening now

_____ The point of view—first-, second-, or third-person—indicated by the form a word takes on in a sentence

_____ A word that represents a person, place, thing, event, or idea

Lesson 5.4
Correcting Misplaced and Dangling Modifiers

OBJECTIVE

★ Identify and correct misplaced and dangling modifiers.

BIG IDEA

Modifiers give additional meaning and clarity to your writing; using them correctly will improve your writing.

Modifiers are words or groups of words that add _____ _____ to a sentence. The most common types of modifiers are **adjectives** and **adverbs**. However, some **phrases** and even some clauses can also be considered modifiers.

This lesson will help you correct two types of incorrect modifiers:

- Misplaced Modifiers
- Dangling Modifiers

Misplaced Modifiers

A **misplaced modifier** is _____ _____ _____ from what it modifies. This makes the sentence potentially _____ to your audience.

Example:

   Rory and Miranda saw the Eiffel Tower <u>honeymooning in Paris</u>.

This modifier is misplaced because it suggests that the Eiffel Tower was honeymooning in Paris.

Dangling Modifiers

In a **dangling modifier**, the word that is being modified is completely _____ from the sentence.

Example:

   Cleaning the garage, a mouse ran across the floor.

You could fix the sentence by adding *who* was cleaning the garage.

   Cleaning the garage, <u>Dad</u> saw a mouse run across the floor.

Rewrite the following sentences so that they no longer have dangling modifiers:

   Sorting through old family pictures, there was a picture of my grandma and me.

   Looking into the sky, an airplane flew overhead.

Making a sandwich, there was no more mustard.

Doing laundry, ran out of detergent.

Running through the streets, scattered everywhere were ducklings.

On Your Own

Which of the following sentences does not contain a misplaced or dangling modifier?

Making the bed, my sheets were untucked at the bottom.

Since announcing his presidential campaign, the phones have been ringing all day.

After finishing the exam, students began collecting their materials.

Lesson Wrap-up

Key Terms

Define the following Key Terms from this lesson.

Adjective:

Adverb:

Complete Sentence:

Dangling Modifier:

Misplaced Modifier:

Modifier:

Phrase:

Lesson 5.5
Using Word and Sentence Variety

OBJECTIVE

★ Learn how to vary words, phrases, and clauses.

BIG IDEA

Using a variety of word and sentence structures in your writing will keep your readers interested and engaged in what you have to say.

In this lesson, you will learn how to introduce more variety into your words, phrases, and clauses.

Words

To avoid repetition in your writing, you should substitute words with _____ and _____.

Pronouns are words that _____ **nouns**. Using pronouns can help you avoid _____ the same noun over and over again.

Another strategy for introducing new words into your writing is using synonyms. **Synonyms** are words that share the _____ meaning as other words.

List **synonyms** for the following words.

happy:

warm:

afraid:

tired:

mad:

On Your Own

Read the paragraph and, in the following table, list the synonyms it uses for the word *home*.

> Janice has always wanted to own a home of her own. When she was seven, her father lost his job, and her parents were unable to make payments on the family's house. As a result, Janice found herself staying in the apartments of other relatives, moving from residence to residence every few weeks. To Janice, a home is more than a building: it's a symbol of security and safety.

Synonyms for *home*

Phrases

Another strategy for using variety in your writing is replacing _____ words with descriptive _____.

You can also add new phrases to the _____ of a sentence to add _____ and interest.

Remember that any time you add a phrase to the beginning of a sentence, you must add a _____.

Add a phrase to the independent clauses below to add interest to each sentence:

<u>Coming in late and talking</u>, Marlene disrupts the class every day.

_____, he spotted a herd of deer in the field.

_____, the birds were noisy.

Clauses

A final way that you can add interest to your writing is varying the _____ of your _____.

Use a coordinating conjunction to join each pair of independent clauses. (To remember the coordinating conjunctions, remember the acronym FANBOYS.)

Sarah didn't like the movie, _____ she left early.

My car got hit in the parking lot, _____ I called the police and my insurance company.

I hated plucking chickens when I was a kid, _____ my dad made me do it anyway.

Now, use a semicolon to join each pair of independent clauses.

I will need to buy some new clothes   I have lost a lot of weight.

He has to get up early in the morning   he will go to bed by 9:00 p.m.

On Your Own

Read the following paragraph and look for ways to add word and sentence variety. Then, use the space below to rewrite the paragraph with your changes.

> The most significant result of the Boston Tea Party and the Intolerable Acts was the formation of the Continental Congress. In 1774, fifty-five men met in Philadelphia, PA, to discuss the Boston Tea Party and the Intolerable Acts. Some of the notable men were Samuel Adams, George Washington, and Patrick Henry. The men met for seven weeks. John Adams convinced the men of the need for a confederation. He stressed, above all, unification of purpose within the colonies. The first Continental Congress did not directly support a revolution. The Continental Congress laid the framework for a revolution by unifying the colonies. The Continental Congress also drew up documents such as the Declaration of Rights.

Lesson Wrap-up

Key Terms

Beside each definition, write the corresponding term.

_____ : A word that describes a noun or pronoun

_____ : A word that describes a verb, an adjective, or another adverb

_____ : A punctuation mark used to separate items in a list; join compound sentences; mark introductory words, phrases, and

Lesson Wrap-up

_____: clauses; add extra or unnecessary details to a sentence; and separate similar adjectives

_____: A sentence that contains at least one subject and one verb and expresses a complete thought

_____: Two independent clauses joined by a comma and a conjunction

_____: A conjunction that connects words or word groups of equal importance in a sentence

_____: A word group that contains a subject and a verb but does not express a complete thought

_____: A group of words with a subject and a verb that expresses a complete thought

_____: A word that represents a person, place, thing, event, or idea

_____: A short piece of writing that focuses on one main idea

_____: A word group that adds to the meaning of a sentence but does not form a complete thought and usually lacks a subject and a verb

_____: A word that takes the place of a noun in a sentence

_____: A punctuation mark used to combine two independent clauses and separate long list items

_____: A sentence made up of one independent clause

_____: A conjunction that introduces a dependent clause

_____: A word that has the same meaning as another word

_____: A word that describes a noun or pronoun

_____: A word that describes a verb, an adjective, or another adverb

_____: A punctuation mark used to separate items in a list; join compound sentences; mark introductory words, phrases, and clauses; add extra or unnecessary details to a sentence; and separate similar adjectives

_____: A sentence that contains at least one subject and one verb and expresses a complete thought

_____: Two independent clauses joined by a comma and a conjunction

_____: A conjunction that connects words or word groups of equal importance in a sentence

_____: A word group that contains a subject and a verb but does not express a complete thought

_____: A group of words with a subject and a verb that expresses a complete thought

Lesson 5.6
Using Parallelism, Coordination, and Subordination

OBJECTIVES

★ Apply methods for combining ideas.
★ Define and identify parallelism, coordination, and subordination.
★ Evaluate sentence structures.

BIG IDEA

When you write, one of your main goals should be to show connections between ideas. The way that you structure a sentence can help establish those relationships and make your writing flow smoothly.

In this lesson, you will learn three ways to add structure to your writing:

- Coordination
- Subordination
- Parallelism

Coordination

Coordination is used to _____ two related ideas. To combine sentences of equal importance, you can use a _____ and a _____ _____.

Example:

  Brian is an Italian food connoisseur. He enjoys French food even more.
  Brian is an Italian food connoisseur, but he enjoys French cuisine even more.

Instead of a comma and coordinating conjunction, you can also use a _____.

Subordination

Subordination is used to connect related ideas of _____ importance.

Insert a subordinating conjunction in each of the following sentences to complete the subordinate clause:

  _____ I go shopping, my sister always wants to see what I've bought.

  I fall down _____ I wear those shoes.

  Will you watch my dog _____ I am finished with my homework?

  _____ he is wealthy, he never spends any money.

Parallelism

In writing, parallelism is used to create _____ between two or more _____ ideas by using similarly-structured _____, _____, or _____.

Examples:

My brother <u>watches</u> TV, <u>rides</u> his bike, and <u>hangs</u> out with his friends.

All my brother does is <u>watch</u> TV, <u>ride</u> his bike, and <u>hang</u> out with his friends.

On Your Own

Use the following list items in a sentence. You may need to change the wording.

seeing new movies   music recommendations   watch old TV shows

On Your Own

Identify the list item that doesn't seem to fit with the others in each sentence:

1. My favorite hobbies include playing the guitar, watching action movies, and anything with basketball.
2. The committee resolved to cut funding for after-school programs, decided to hold nominations for a new chairperson, and interviewing the recently hired police chief.

Lesson Wrap-up

Key Terms

Define the following Key Terms from this lesson.

Comma:

Compound Sentence:

Coordinating Conjunction:

Coordination:

Conjunction:

Independent Clause:

Paragraph:

Parallelism:

Phrase:

Semicolon:

Subordinating Conjunction:

Subordination:

Lesson 5.7
Using Active and Passive Voice

OBJECTIVE

★ Understand the differences between active and passive voice.

BIG IDEA

Learning to find a good balance of active and passive voice will help you refine your writing skills and communicate your ideas better.

This lesson will teach you how to use both active and passive voice.

Active Voice

When a sentence uses **active voice**, the **subject** is _____ an action.

Complete each sentence with an action the underlined subject is performing.

The <u>raccoon</u> _____.

Ever since I saw that scary movie, <u>I've</u> _____.

Whenever I'm away, my <u>dog</u> _____.

On Your Own

Read the following sentences and identify the one using active voice.

Our entire road was paved by the crew last week.

The kitchen will be cleaned by your brother every Wednesday.

The mischievous puppy ate three socks in one day.

Passive Voice

When a sentence is in **passive voice**, the **subject** is _____ an action.

Sentences in passive voice contain the correct form of the **helping verb** "_____ _____" in addition to a **past participle**.

In your writing, passive voice can sound both _____ and _____.

Passive voice can also confuse your audience when the person or object _____ the action is not _____ in the sentence.

On Your Own

Rewrite the following passive sentences so that they use active voice.

The entire yard was raked by Sarah.

The video was posted on Facebook by an anonymous source.

Instructions will be read to you by the teaching assistant.

The book was written by a best-selling author.

Reasons for using passive voice:

Keeping an emphasis on a word other than the _____.

To keep the meaning of a sentence purposefully _____.

To add sentence _____ to a text.

Lesson Wrap-up

Key Terms

Define the following Key Terms from this lesson.

Active Voice:

Helping Verb:

Paragraph:

Passive Voice:

Past Participle:

Subject:

Verb:

Lesson 5.8
Emphasizing Words or Phrases

OBJECTIVE

★ Learn how to place emphasis on words or phrases in a sentence.

BIG IDEA

You can use words and structures to emphasize the most important details in your writing.

In this lesson, you will learn three ways to emphasize important words or phrases:

- Subordination
- Word Order
- Sentence Structure

Subordination

Usually, the main **subject** and **verb** are the most _____ words in a sentence. They express the most _____ ideas. Less important ideas should be **subordinated**, or _____, in **dependent clauses.**

On Your Own

Read the following passage and identify the sentence that uses subordination.

> The famous pirate Blackbeard blockaded the port of Charleston, South Carolina, in 1718. He demanded medical supplies in exchange for the safe return of a group of prisoners. After the exchange was delayed, the pirates moved several ships into the harbor. The city was alarmed by this; Blackbeard's reputation made every coastal city fear him.

Word Order

Important information shouldn't be _____ in the middle of a sentence. You can make this information more _____ by placing it at the beginning or end of a sentence.

Similarly, you can emphasize **phrases** by moving them to the beginning of a sentence. By _____ the subject and verb of the sentence, you can _____ a feeling of suspense in your audience.

Sentence Structure

The third way to emphasize ideas is by using a _____ or

_____ sentence structure. These sentences _____

_____ to the audience because they are different from the rest of the text.

Test Yourself

Identify the most important idea in each of the following sentences.

Even though you have been busy, you still should've called me.

Twirling gracefully in the fall breeze, the leaves reminded me of little ballerinas.

After careful consideration, I have decided not to take the job in London.

Whenever my mother-in-law comes around, I feel like I have been judged on my child rearing and my housekeeping.

The position of lead scientist will be given to the employee who has shown the most dedication to this company.

Lesson Wrap-up

Key Terms

Write the letter for each term next to its definition.

a) Dependent Clause
b) Independent Clause
c) Phrase
d) Subject
e) Subordinating Conjunction
f) Subordination
g) Verb

_____ A word group that contains a subject and a verb and expresses a complete thought

_____ The person, place, thing, event, or idea a sentence is about

_____ A stylistic method for de-emphasizing an idea in a combined sentence

_____ A word that represents an action, relationship, or state of being

_____ A word group that contains a subject and a verb but does not express a complete thought

_____ A word group that adds meaning to a sentence but does not express a complete thought and usually lacks a subject and a verb

_____ A conjunction that introduces a dependent clause

Lesson 5.9
Choosing Clear, Concise, and Vivid Words

OBJECTIVE

★ Understand the characteristics of clear, concise, and vivid words.

BIG IDEA

To make a situation as exciting as possible, you have to include vivid descriptions and fascinating details. However, language that is too flowery or complicated might distract your audience from the main idea. Balancing these two extremes is essential for becoming a good storyteller.

In this lesson, you will learn how to effectively communicate meaning with the following word choices:

- Clear Words
- Concise Words
- Vivid Words

Clear Words

Strong writing is _____ and easy to _____.

While academic and professional documents may be _____, they should not be _____.

One specific type of unclear language is **jargon**, or _____ _____ terms.
Generally, you should avoid jargon unless you are writing for a _____ **audience**.

Concise Words

Concise word choice eliminates _____ _____ from your writing.

On Your Own

In the following table, write more concise versions of the three wordy phrases from the passage below.

> I wanted to see if you would be willing to meet with me for just a couple minutes tomorrow in the afternoon at 2:15 or sometime around then. I would really appreciate being able to hear what you think about the progress I've made with the first draft of the paper that I've been writing. Due to the fact that I am having some trouble with organizing my paragraphs, I am hoping that you can help me. It would be great if I could come to your office after class tomorrow afternoon, but I can also meet at another time if it would work better for you.

Wordy	Concise
just a couple minutes tomorrow in the afternoon at 2:15 or sometime around then	
the first draft of the paper I've been writing	
Due to the fact that I am having some trouble with organizing my paragraphs	

Vivid Words

The final aspect of word choice is using _____ language. When you are sharing information with your audience, you want your words to be _____ and _____.

Nouns and Action Verbs

In the following table, write vivid versions of the vague nouns and verbs

Vague Noun	Vivid Noun	Vague Verb	Vivid Verb
baby		walking	
park		talking	
picture		eating	
animal		running	

Adjectives and Adverbs

In the following table, write vivid versions of the vague adjectives and adverbs.

Vague Adjective	Vivid Adjective	Vague Adverb	Vivid Adverb
pretty		very	
happy		really	
serious		bravely	
cold		blindly	

Lesson Wrap-up

Key Terms

Define the following Key Terms from this lesson.

Action Verb:

Active Voice:

Adjective:

Adverb:

Audience:

Formality:

Jargon:

Main Idea:

Noun:

Phrase:

Subject:

Synonym:

Verb:

Lesson 5.10
Using Inclusive Language

OBJECTIVES

★ Identify exclusive language.
★ Understand the importance of inclusive language.

BIG IDEA

By becoming familiar with the differences between inclusive and exclusive language, you can ensure that your writing is respectful and sensitive to others.

In this lesson, you will learn to use language that is inclusive based on the following factors:

- Gender
- Ethnicity or Culture
- Physical or Mental Ability
- Sexual Orientation

Gender

In the past, society has used **gender-specific** words like *mankind* to describe both _____ and _____. This language is considered _____ because it refers specifically to men even though the group includes women. In these instances, it would be better to use a **gender-neutral** term like _____.

Instead of defaulting to a certain _____, use the term *he or she*.

You can also make the _____ _____ so that you can use the plural, gender-neutral pronoun *they*.

Add the correct, gender-neutral personal pronoun to the following sentences.

If someone needs to leave the office early today, _____ or _____ will need to talk to the vice president first.

If the managers need to leave the office early today, _____ will need to talk to the vice president first.

Ethnicity or Culture

Inclusive language does not make _____ about people based on their _____ or _____.

Physical or Mental Ability

A person's _____ or _____ abilities do not _____ them. Just like gender or ethnicity, a person's physical or mental abilities should only be _____ if this information is _____ to your purpose.

Sexual Orientation

If a person's sexual orientation is irrelevant to the sentence, don't _____ it. When you do need to reference someone's sexual orientation, always use terms that are _____.

Lesson Wrap-up

Key Terms

Define the following Key Terms from this lesson.

Credibility:

Exclusive Language:

Gender-Neutral:

Gender-Specific:

Inclusive Language:

Paragraph:

Personal Pronoun:

Pronoun:

Lesson 5.11
Proofreading Sentences for Style

OBJECTIVES

- ★ Learn a process for proofreading for style.
- ★ Proofread a sentence to correct confusion over pronoun antecedents.
- ★ Proofread a sentence to correct errors in verb tense.
- ★ Proofread a sentence to correctly punctuate subordinate clauses.

BIG IDEA

Learning to proofread for sentence style will help you express your ideas in the best possible way. That extra polish might be just what you need to earn a higher grade, impress a hiring manager, or convince a skeptical audience.

In this lesson, you will learn how to proofread a text for style issues.

Review Writing Style Guidelines

Proofreading Checklist: Sentence Style

- ✓ Meaning: _____

- ✓ Delivery: _____

- ✓ Consistency: _____

Proofread in Stages

During each proofreading stage, focus on just _____ style _____ at a time.

Try Multiple Reading Techniques

One of the best ways to proofread for style is reading your work _____ to yourself. It can help you hear _____ sentences, _____ problems, and inconsistent _____.

Get a Second Opinion

When you read your own writing multiple times, you will slowly get used to the _____ and _____ of your sentences.

Ask a _____ or family member to review your text and give you _____.

Take Frequent Breaks

Taking a break from your paper is _____ when proofreading for style.

To make sure that you have enough time to review your work thoroughly, schedule proofreading time in your _____.

You should spread these times across _____ days.

Lesson Wrap-up

Key Terms

Define the following Key Terms from this lesson.

Active Voice:

Audience:

Parallelism:

Sequential Learning:

Tense:

Verb:

Chapter 6
Writing Paragraphs

Lesson 6.1
The Writing Process for Paragraphs

OBJECTIVE
★ Identify the stages in writing a paragraph.

BIG IDEA
Using the academic writing process will ensure that you write a focused paragraph.

The **academic writing process** breaks up an assignment into five stages:

1.
2.
3.
4.
5.

All five stages are _____ to the writing process. While skipping a step might save you time in the _____ _____, you will have to spend time fixing or even re-writing your paragraph later.

As you use the academic writing process, don't be afraid to circle back to a _____ stage.

This lesson will review the academic writing process for paragraphs.

Pre-Writing

Define the term **pre-writing**.

Lesson 6.1 | The Writing Process for Paragraphs

What does the pre-writing step of the writing process involve?

Goals of Pre-writing

What are the questions you answer during the pre-writing stage?

1.

2.

3.

On Your Own

In the following example, is Mario pre-writing? Check the box next to your answer.

> Mario reviews the guidelines given to him by his history instructor for a major paper. He then brainstorms possible topics for his history paper on the Civil War. After that, he is going to the library to search the databases for information about the Civil War.
>
> ☐ Yes
> ☐ No

Drafting

During the second step in the writing process, _____, you will start _____ out your ideas.

While you are drafting:

Don't worry too much about _____ or _____.

Focus on the _____ that you want to cover.

You can always make _____ and _____ later.

Drafting involves writing your _____ _____ and your _____ _____. These sentences should _____ on the information presented in your _____ _____.

Revising

_____ is the third stage in the writing process.

During this stage, you will:

Add and remove _____.

_____-_____ your sentences to make sure you are _____ your ideas clearly.

You may also participate in _____ _____ or receive feedback from your _____.

The revising stage is usually broken into two parts:
1. Revising for Content:
   Look for _____ _____.

   Include all the _____ details.

2. Revising for Organization:
   Make sure the sentences are in _____ _____.

   Add, delete, or _____-_____ a sentence if it makes your paragraph easier to understand.

Editing

_____ is the fourth stage in the writing process.

This stage involves fixing _____, _____, and _____ issues.

Focus on one _____ of error at a time. You may want to _____ the editing process into more than one _____.

On Your Own

In the following example, is the advice of Ingrid's friend correct? Check the box next to your answer.

Ingrid is having trouble finding the errors in a press release for her marketing class. Her friend suggests re-reading her paragraph several times while looking for a different type of writing error each time.

☐ Yes
☐ No

Submitting

The last stage in the writing process is _____ your work. This is an opportunity to _____ your work with its _____.

During the submitting stage, you will _____ your paragraph.

You might format the text in _____ (Modern Language Association) Style. MLA style is a method for _____ and _____ academic writing.

Lesson Wrap-up

Test Yourself

Next to each statement, write **T** for True or **F** for False. Check your work using the Answer Key in the back of the book.

1. _____ All paragraphs must be eight to ten sentences long.
2. _____ If the ideas in a paragraph aren't focused, the audience won't be able to follow them.
3. _____ There are six stages in the academic writing process.
4. _____ It's okay to skip a step to save time.
5. _____ You can move back and forth between different steps of the writing process.
6. _____ Drafting is the first step of the academic writing process.
7. _____ You can skip the pre-writing stage.
8. _____ Pay attention to grammar and spelling during the drafting stage.
9. _____ Drafting involves writing support sentences and a concluding sentence.
10. _____ Revising is generally broken into two parts: content and organization.

Key Terms

Define the following Key Terms from this lesson.

Academic Writing Process:

Audience:

Concluding Sentence:

Drafting:

Editing:

Global Learning:

Main Idea:

MLA:

Organizational Pattern:

Paragraph:

Pre-writing:

Purpose:

Revising:

Sequential Learning:

Submitting:

Support Sentence:

Topic Sentence:

Writing Center:

Lesson 6.2
Choosing a Topic and Scope for a Paragraph

OBJECTIVES
- ★ Identify strategies for choosing a topic.
- ★ Understand the importance of narrowing the scope of a topic.

BIG IDEA

Carefully considering the topic of a paragraph will ensure that your writing is clear and focused.

The first step in _____-_____ a paragraph is selecting a _____.

Define the term **topic**.

Without a topic, the _____ of your writing will be _____.

This lesson will teach you three useful steps in choosing a topic and narrowing your scope:
- Review the Assignment Directions
- Use Brainstorming Strategies
- Think about Audience, Purpose, and Constraints

Review the Assignment Directions

Define the term **writing prompt**.

What four questions should you ask yourself when reviewing assignment directions?

1.
2.
3.
4.

On Your Own

Read the following prompts, paying close attention to the assignment guidelines. Then, in the space below, write your own prompt for an assignment in one of your classes.

> Write a well-developed paragraph about your learning style. Make sure you have a topic sentence and supporting details. The writing rubric located in the Course Information tab will be used to grade the paragraph. Turn in the typed paragraph on Monday.

Enforcing term limits is a procedure where the number of terms an individual may hold an elected office is set by law. For example, the President of the United States may not serve more than two terms. Research the issue to better understand the potential positive and negative effects of term limits. Then, write an argumentative, five-paragraph essay explaining your position and supporting it with information from scholarly articles. Use MLA style.

On Your Own

In the following example, is Juan's friend correct? Check the box next to your answer.

Juan is having trouble understanding a writing assignment in his history class. Juan's friend suggests highlighting any special guideline as he re-reads the writing prompt.

☐ Yes
☐ No

Writing prompts also include _____ _____ that tell you what type of paragraph to write.

Write the definition for each key word:

Analyze:

Define:

Discuss:

Evaluate:

Lesson 6.2 | Choosing a Topic and Scope for a Paragraph

Identify:

Prove:

Share:

Summarize:

On Your Own

Read the following writing prompts and identify the key word in each.

> Several styles of parenting have been covered in class. Write a paragraph sharing the parenting style your parents used with you.

> Write a paragraph proving two triangles are congruent.

Use Brainstorming Strategies

You can use _____ strategies to explore what you might want to _____ in your paragraph.

What are two questions to think about as you brainstorm?

1.

2.

Lists

Listing involves writing down _____ _____ and phrase that comes to mind during a set period of time.

To start listing, follow these steps:

1.

2.

3.

Mind Maps

A _____ _____ helps you see relationships between ideas. To create one, follow these steps:

1.

2.

3.

On Your Own

Now, try mind mapping on your own. Create a mind map on the topic "terrorism" in the blank mind map below. When you're done, look at the example mind map in the lesson and see how your ideas compare.

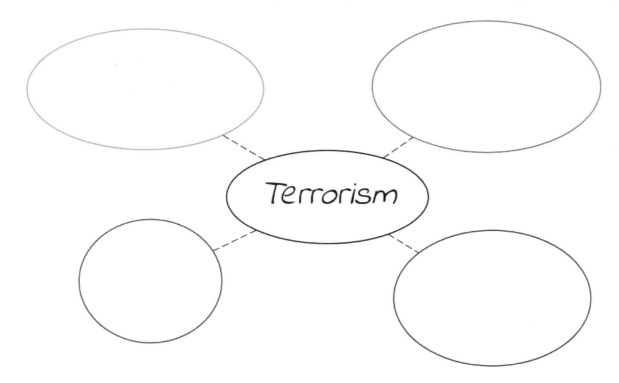

Think about Audience, Purpose, and Constraints

Define the term **scope.**

What are some questions to ask yourself when considering your audience, purpose, and constraints?

1.

2.

3.

Lesson 6.2 | Choosing a Topic and Scope for a Paragraph

First, think about the _____ of your paragraph.

Define the most common purposes for writing.

To inform:

To persuade:

To reflect:

To entertain:

_____ is another important factor to consider when you are narrowing the scope of your topic. Your **audience** is the group of people who will read your **paragraph**.

What questions can you ask yourself as you think about your audience?

1.
   a.
   b.
   c.
2.
   a.
   b.
   c.

On Your Own

Complete the table below, determining the audience for each text.

Text	Audience
Report for work	
Personal blog entry	
An accident report for insurance	
Text message	
Paper for history class	

Lesson Wrap-up

Key Terms

Define the following Key Terms from this lesson.

Active Learning:

Audience:

Brainstorming:

Constraint:

Entertaining Text:

Focus:

Informative Text:

Listing:

Mind Mapping:

Narrowed Topic:

Paragraph:

Persuasive Text:

Pre-writing:

Purpose:

Reflective Text:

Scope:

Visual Learning:

Writing Prompt:

Lesson 6.3
Writing a Topic Sentence

OBJECTIVES

★ Recognize strong controlling ideas for specific purposes.
★ Recognize the characteristics of a good topic sentence.
★ Understand the differences between a topic and a controlling idea.

BIG IDEA

A clear and concise topic sentence is the foundation for a good paragraph. It guides you and your audience through your writing.

In this lesson, you will learn how to draft an effective topic sentence by reading about the following:

- Characteristics of a Topic Sentence
- Determining a Controlling Idea
- Constructing the Topic Sentence

Characteristics of a Topic Sentence

A topic sentence should be a _____, not a question.

    Topic sentences are always _____-_____ statements that tell the reader exactly what to expect in a _____.

    If you want to include a thought-provoking question in your writing, place it _____ or _____ your topic sentence.

A topic sentence should be _____ and _____.

    Your topic sentence introduces your _____ on a topic.

    Using _____ phrases like "_____ _____" or "_____ _____" will weaken your _____ and potentially confuse your _____.

A topic sentence should be written in your _____ _____.

    You can still use an interesting _____ or _____ in your paragraph; just put it _____ or _____ your topic sentence.

On Your Own

Identify which of the following topic sentences is strongest.

    College tuition is too high, forcing most students to take on overwhelming student loans.

Why is college tuition so high?

According to The Money Tracker, college tuition has risen at least 20% a year for the last five years.

Determining a Controlling Idea

To write a _____ _____, you need to decide on a controlling idea for your paragraph.

Define the term **controlling idea**.

Your controlling idea is always influenced by the _____ of your paragraph.

On Your Own

For each purpose, fill in your own controlling ideas about the topic "rising food costs" in the table below.

Purpose	Controlling Idea
To inform	
To persuade	
To reflect	
To entertain	

Constructing the Topic Sentence

_____ + _____ _____ = Topic Sentence

The strongest controlling idea fits all the requirements of a good topic sentence:

1.

2.

3.

Lesson 6.3 | Writing a Topic Sentence

Complete the following chart by adding a controlling idea and topic sentence for each topic. Remember to determine your purpose.

Topic	Controlling Idea	Topic Sentence
My favorite hobby		
Applying for college		
The effects of social media		

Lesson Wrap-up

Key Terms

Define the following Key Terms from this lesson.

Academic Writing Process:

Audience:

Controlling Idea:

Entertaining Text:

Informative Text:

Narrowed Topic:

Paragraph:

Persuasive Text:

Purpose:

Reflective Text:

Supporting Detail:

Topic Sentence:

Lesson 6.4
Choosing an Organizational Pattern

OBJECTIVES
- ★ Identify different types of organizational patterns.
- ★ Recognize appropriate transitions.
- ★ Recognize characteristics of organizational patterns.

BIG IDEA

Organizational patterns help you stay on track while writing and help your audience better understand your ideas.

In this lesson, you will learn the characteristics of six organizational patterns:

- Cause and Effect
- Chronological
- Compare and Contrast
- Order of Importance
- Spatial
- Topical

Cause and Effect

A **cause and effect** paragraph discusses the _____ and/or _____ of a topic.

This organizational pattern works well for both _____ and _____ paragraphs.

Transitions are _____, _____, or _____ that show order and make _____ between ideas.

List three transition words or phrases for a cause and effect paragraph:

1.
2.
3.

Chronological

A **chronological** paragraph shares ideas or events in the _____ that they occurred.

Lesson 6.4 | Choosing an Organizational Pattern

This type of organizational pattern works well in paragraphs meant to _____ the audience about a historical event or _____ the audience with an interesting story.

List three transition words or phrases for a chronological paragraph:

1.
2.
3.

On Your Own

Read the examples below and identify the passage that is written chronologically.

Last, going with the natural grain of the wood, apply the stain in an even layer. First, use sandpaper to smooth the wood and remove the existing varnish. Next, clean the surface with mineral spirits.

First, use sandpaper to smooth the wood and remove the existing varnish. Last, going with the natural grain of the wood, apply the stain in an even layer. Next, clean the surface with mineral spirits.

First, use sandpaper to smooth the wood and remove the existing varnish. Next, clean the surface with mineral spirits. Last, going with the natural grain of the wood, apply the stain in an even layer.

Compare and Contrast

The **compare and contrast** organizational pattern is used for paragraphs that discuss the _____ and _____ between two topics.

List three transition words or phrases for a compare and contrast paragraph:

1.
2.
3.

Order of Importance

A paragraph arranged in **order of importance** organizes the information from _____ to _____ _____ or vice versa.

© HAWKES LEARNING

Spatial 237

This organizational pattern is often used to _____ a point in a _____ paragraph.

List three transition words or phrases for an order of importance paragraph:

1.
2.
3.

On Your Own

Read the following sentences and identify the transition words or phrases.

> The most important step in constructing a well-built house is using quality building materials. For contractors, hiring professional workers is an equally important consideration.

Spatial

A **spatial** paragraph describes a _____ or _____ by its _____ characteristics.

The description in a spatially ordered paragraph usually moves from one _____ to the _____ in an _____ way.

The spatial organizational pattern works well when your purpose is to _____ or _____.

On Your Own

In the space below, use spatial organization to write a short description of your current location.

Topical

Topical paragraphs are not arranged in a _____ order because all of the information is of _____ _____.

© HAWKES LEARNING

Lesson 6.4 | Choosing an Organizational Pattern

This pattern is sometimes referred to as "_____" and is often used for _____ or _____ writing.

Write the usual structure of a topical paragraph:

-
-
-
-
-

List three transition words or phrases for a topical paragraph:

1.
2.
3.

On Your Own

Determine what type of organizational pattern is used in the following paragraph and check the box next to your answer.

When baking a cherry pie, begin by placing a ready-made pie crust in a nine-inch pie plate. Next, add a can of cherry pie filling to the crust. After spreading out the cherries, place a second crust on the top of the filling. Finally, bake the pie at 400 degrees for about an hour.

☐ Cause and Effect
☐ Chronological
☐ Order of Importance
☐ Spatial

Lesson Wrap-up

Key Terms

Beside each definition, write the corresponding term.

_____: A word, phrase, or sentence that shows order and makes connections between ideas

_____: An organizational pattern used to explain the causes or effects of a topic

_____: An organizational pattern used to describe a topic by its physical characteristics

_____: An organizational pattern used to show the similarities and differences between two topics

_____: A text that convinces its audience to adopt a belief or take an action

_____: A text that gives the audience information about a topic

_____: The structure of a written text, used to arrange the main points of a work

_____: A general organizational pattern used for equally important main points

_____: A text that shares a personal experience or belief

_____: A short piece of writing that focuses on one main idea

_____: An organizational pattern that arranges information in order of importance

_____: A text that explores a topic or event in a creative or humorous way

_____: An organizational pattern that arranges ideas or events in the order that they occurred

Lesson 6.5
Drafting a Paragraph

OBJECTIVES

★ Identify types of transitions and their uses.
★ Recognize the eight types of supporting details.
★ Recognize the structure of a paragraph.
★ Understand the drafting process.

BIG IDEA

Drafting is when you put your ideas together and organize them effectively. The focus should be on building a solid paragraph, not perfecting your grammar and spelling.

In this lesson, you will learn three important elements of a first draft:

- Support Sentences
- Concluding Sentences
- Transitions

Support Sentences

Support sentences _____ and _____ your topic sentence. They can build your _____, explain a _____ topic, or tell a _____.

Your **organizational pattern** determines the _____ of the main points in your paragraph.

Supporting details are pieces of information that make your paragraph more _____ and _____ by expanding on your _____ _____.

List the seven types of supporting details:

1.   5.
2.   6.
3.   7.

Any supporting details that you include in your paragraph must be introduced and explained in your own words through _____ _____.

On Your Own

Read the following passage and determine the type of supporting detail it uses. Check the box next to your answer.

It's crucial that states develop better programs for providing children with adequate clothing. When I was ten, my family couldn't afford to buy me winter shoes. Instead, I wore gym shoes as I stood in a foot of snow at the bus stop every day. Eventually, my feet became frostbitten, and I missed school for a week. Worse, I almost lost some of my toes.

☐ Expert Analysis ☐ Statistic
☐ Fact ☐ Anecdote
☐ Reflection

Concluding Sentences

Your concluding sentence ends the paragraph by _____ the ideas you just _____.

Often, the concluding sentence also _____ the topic sentence using _____ words.

On Your Own

Read the following topic sentence.

The libraries of today use digital technologies to provide many services that were traditionally completed by hand.

Identify the concluding sentence that best restates the topic sentence.

Libraries provide a variety of services.

Modern libraries use electronic resources rather than traditional paper and pencils for many of their services.

Computer labs can be found at most modern libraries.

Your _____ for writing will also influence the _____ of concluding sentence that fits your _____ best.

What are two questions you can ask yourself to think of ideas for your concluding sentence?

1.

2.

Transitions

Define the term **transition.**

Transitions give your audience _____ that they can use to follow the _____ of your _____.

What are the two main types of transition words?

1.
2.

Complete the following table with the transition words provided in the lesson.

Order	Connections

On Your Own

Read the following sentences and identify the one that uses a stronger transition word.

I need to deposit my check; likewise, the bank is closed.

I need to deposit my check; however, the bank is closed.

Lesson Wrap-up

Key Terms

Define the following Key Terms from this lesson.

Academic Writing:

Academic Writing Process:

Anecdote:

Audience:

Cause and Effect:

Compare and Contrast:

Concluding Sentence:

Description:

Drafting:

Editing:

Example:

Expert Analysis:

Fact:

First Draft:

Informative Text:

Main Idea:

Organizational Pattern:

Paragraph:

Persuasive Text:

Purpose:

Reflection:

Statistic:

Support Sentence:

Supporting Detail:

Topic Sentence:

Transition:

Lesson 6.6
Revising and Editing a Paragraph

OBJECTIVE

★ Learn a process for revising a paragraph.

BIG IDEA

Revising helps you focus on content, not grammar. Once you have revised the ideas in your paragraph, you can start editing.

In this lesson, you will learn about the third and fourth stages of the writing process:
- Revising Ideas
- Editing Words and Sentences

Revising Ideas

Focus

A **focused** paragraph:
- ☐ Clearly communicates its _____ _____
- ☐ Uses every sentence to _____ and _____ that idea

On Your Own

Read the following paragraph and identify the sentence that should be deleted to make the paragraph more focused.

> When I was growing up, my brother was the most important person in my life. My brother was important to me for three reasons. First, he was my best friend. We did everything together; we even went to summer camp together. Second, he could already drive. I wouldn't have been able to go anywhere if he wasn't willing to take me. I couldn't wait to get my own license. The third reason my brother was important is that he was the drummer in my band. I could sing, but he was the one who kept us on-beat. My brother played a vital role in my childhood.

List the four questions you can ask yourself as you revise for focus:

1.
2.
3.
4.

Development

A well-developed paragraph:
- ☐ Presents information in an _____ way
- ☐ Includes plenty of _____ to support its _____ _____

Editing Words and Sentences 245

On Your Own

Take a look at this paragraph from earlier in the lesson. The highlighted sentence has been added; does it strengthen the paragraph's development? Check the box next to your answer.

> When I was growing up, my brother was the most important person in my life. My brother was important to me for three reasons. First, he was my best friend. We did everything together; we even went to summer camp together. Second, he could already drive. **My brother took me to school every morning and band practice every afternoon.** I wouldn't have been able to go anywhere if he wasn't willing to take me. I couldn't wait to get my own license. The third reason my brother was important is that he was the drummer in my band. I could sing, but he was the one who kept us on-beat. My brother played a vital role in my childhood.

☐ Yes   ☐ No

What questions should you ask yourself as you revise for development?

1.   4.
2.   5.
3.

Revision Strategies

List the strategies for effective revision:

1.   3.
2.   4.

Editing Words and Sentences

Editing involves proofreading your work to make sure the writing is completely free of _____, _____, and _____ errors.

List the strategies that will help you become an effective editor:

Start at the _____.

Know your _____ _____.

Look for _____ _____ at a time.

On Your Own

Locate five errors in the following paragraph:

In mathematics, knowing weather to calculate the area or perimeter of a shape is essential. Calculate the area of a shape. When you want to determine the number of square units the shape occupies. In real life, area was used in situations such as calculating the amount of flooring needed for a new home. Perimeter, on the other hand, is used to calculate the length of the boundary of a shape. For example, perimeter is used too calculate the amount of fencing needed to enclose a playground. Consider the context of the situation before making the choice between area or perimeter.

Lesson Wrap-up

Key Terms

Define the following Key Terms from this lesson.

Academic Writing Process:

Audience:

Concluding Sentence:

Development:

Drafting:

Editing:

Focus:

Main Idea:

Organizational Pattern:

Paragraph:

Purpose:

Revising:

Supporting Detail:

Topic Sentence:

Transition:

Writing Center:

Lesson 6.7
Submitting a Paragraph

OBJECTIVE

★ Understand how to submit a paragraph.

BIG IDEA

Submitting your work is an opportunity to share your ideas with your audience and reflect on all of the hard work that went into your writing.

In this lesson, you will learn two steps for submitting a paragraph:
- Choose a Format
- Print or Upload Your Work

Choose a Format

Format can involve any of the following details:

-
-
-
-
-
-

On Your Own

Read the following writing prompt and identify the sentences that describe formatting requirements.

> A term limit is a law that sets the maximum number of times an individual may hold an elected office. For example, the president of the United States cannot serve more than two four-year terms. People hold varying opinions on term limits; some believe that term limits prevent political corruption while others think they prevent politicians from thinking about long-term issues. Research the history of term limits to better understand the potential positive and negative effects. Then, write an essay explaining your position on the topic. Your paragraph should be double-spaced and in 12-point Times New Roman font. Remember to set page margins at one inch on all sides.

Print or Upload Your Work

Print your work at least _____ _____ before the due date.

Lesson 6.7 | Submitting a Paragraph

Look over your printed copy one last time before _____ it.

If you email your writing, double check any _____ to make sure you are using the correct file format.

Before sending your document, _____ it to yourself so that you can _____ the file and make sure it opens without any issues.

Check your Sent folder to _____ that the email was delivered without any problems.

On Your Own

Why is it important to print, submit, and/or email an assignment at least one day before it is due? Identify the correct answer.

It gives the instructor extra time to read the assignment.

Students who turn work in early receive higher grades.

It gives you extra time in case you have technology issues.

Lesson Wrap-up

Key Terms

Define the following Key Terms from this lesson.

Academic Writing Process:

Audience:

Editing:

Font:

Format:

Page Margin:

Paragraph:

Purpose:

Revising:

Submitting:

Writing Prompt:

Chapter 7
Writing Longer Texts

Lesson 7.1
Preparing to Write a Longer Text

OBJECTIVES
- ★ Identify the stages in writing a longer text.
- ★ Use a writing schedule to keep a longer text on-track.

BIG IDEA

The academic writing process along with an organized writing schedule will help you as you plan for and work on longer writing assignments.

The _____ _____ _____ is used not only for **paragraphs**, but also for writing research papers or long essays.

This process breaks up a large assignment into five smaller, more manageable stages:

1.
2.
3.
4.
5.

This lesson will give you an overview of the academic writing process and teach you how to use a writing schedule to keep your writing on track.

Pre-Writing and Drafting

The first stage of the writing process is _____-_____. During this stage, you will generate ideas and plan the _____ and organization of your work.

Step-by-Step Checklist: Pre-writing

- ✓ _____
- ✓ _____
- ✓ _____
- ✓ _____

Step-by-Step Checklist: Drafting

- ✓ _____
- ✓ _____
- ✓ _____

Revising and Editing

_____ is the third stage of the writing process. During this stage, you will make _____ to the _____ and _____ of the paper, moving back and forth between drafting and revising multiple times.

_____ involves proofreading for _____, _____, and _____ errors. While revision is the time to improve your ideas, editing is the time to improve your words and sentences.

Submitting

The last step in the writing process is _____ your work.

Define the term **submitting**.

Writing Schedules

A _____ _____ is designed to keep you on track when writing a research paper or long essay.

To create a writing schedule:
- First _____

- Mark _____
- Write dates of all _____
- Add _____
- Set _____
- Write _____
- Spread _____
- Take _____

Lesson Wrap-up

Key Terms

Define the following Key Terms from this lesson.

Academic Writing Process:

Conclusion:

Drafting:

Editing:

Focus:

Format:

Introduction:

Outline:

Paragraph:

Planner:

Pre-writing:

Purpose:

Revising:

Scope:

Submitting:

Writing Schedule:

Lesson 7.2
Understanding Genre and Purpose

OBJECTIVES

- ★ Recognize the expectations and conventions of different genres.
- ★ Understand the purposes of a longer text.

BIG IDEA

It's important to be able to write for a variety of different purposes, genres, and environments.

Define the term **genre**.

In this lesson, you will learn three steps:
- Determine Your Purpose for Writing
- Choose an Appropriate Genre
- Think about Expectations and Conventions

Determine Your Purpose for Writing

Define the four common purposes for writing:

To inform:

To persuade:

To reflect:

To entertain:

Choose an Appropriate Genre

Genres of writing can be divided into three main groups:

1.

2.

3.

Think about Expectations and Conventions   253

Complete the following chart with the genres found in the lesson.

Academic Writing	Professional Writing	Personal Writing

Think about Expectations and Conventions

After you have selected your genre, you must also consider the _____ and _____ that are part of that genre.

Once you've determined the _____ of your audience, you can _____ your writing to better meet those expectations.

Tone

Define the term **tone**.

You establish tone through the _____ you use and the _____ you include.

What kind of tone would you expect to encounter in the following examples? Fill out the table below.

Example	Tone
Newspaper article	
Blog post about a favorite hobby	
A letter to a manager of a restaurant after experiencing bad service	

Style

Writing style affects your _____ _____, _____, and _____ _____.

Lesson 7.2 | Understanding Genre and Purpose

In writing assignments, you will generally use a formal style:

- You are expected to sound _____ or _____.

- You should use more _____ sentence structure and _____ terms.

- You should make your writing _____ and _____ to understand.

Grammar

In academic writing, you are expected to follow _____ grammar and _____ rules.

When you write in personal genres like emails or text messages, your grammar can be more _____.

Lesson Wrap-up

Test Yourself

Next to each text, write **I** for Informal or **F** for Formal. Check your work using the Answer Key in the back of the book.

1. _____ Blog post
2. _____ Newspaper article
3. _____ An academic paper
4. _____ A journal entry
5. _____ A published article

Key Terms

Define the following Key Terms from this lesson.

Academic Writing:

Audience:

Complexity:

Contraction:

Entertaining Text:

Formality:

Genre:

Informative Text:

Personal Writing:

Persuasive Text:

Prior Knowledge:

Professional Writing:

Purpose:

Reflective Text:

Simple Sentence:

Slang:

Tone:

Lesson 7.3
Choosing a Topic and Scope for a Longer Text

OBJECTIVES

★ Identify strategies for choosing a topic and narrowing scope.
★ Understand a variety of purposes when writing a longer text.
★ Understand the importance of narrowing the scope of a topic.

BIG IDEA

The scope, or focus, of your topic should be appropriate for the length of your writing. The scope you choose for your topic should be thoroughly addressed in the given length for the assignment.

Define the term **scope.**

In this lesson you will learn three useful steps in choosing a topic and narrowing your scope:

- Review Instructor Guidelines
- Use Brainstorming Strategies
- Think about Purpose, Audience, and Constraints

Review Instructor Guidelines

What are the six questions to ask yourself when you are trying to come up with ideas for a topic?

1.   4.

2.   5.

3.   6.

Use Brainstorming Strategies

Once you've decided on a general topic, you can use _____ strategies to start developing your ideas.

Define the term **free-writing.**

Free-writing

List the steps of free-writing:

1.

2.

3.

On Your Own

Practice free-writing using the following space. Add your topic at the top; then, start a timer. Keep writing down ideas until the timer goes off.

Grouping

Define the term **grouping**.

List the three steps of grouping:

1.

2.

3.

Keep in mind that the writing process is _____; you may need to complete additional rounds of _____ later.

Think about Audience, Purpose, and Constraints

To start narrowing the scope of your text, you must first _____ your _____ for writing.

List the four most common purposes for writing:

1.   3.

2.   4.

The next step in narrowing down a topic is considering your _____.

Define the term **audience**.

One final way to narrow down your topic is to consider possible _____.

Define the term **constraints.**

List some constraints your professor or manager might give you when you have a written assignment:
1.
2.
3.

Lesson Wrap-up

Key Terms

Beside each definition, write the corresponding term.

_____ :	The style and arrangement of a text
_____ :	Exploring and developing ideas
_____ :	A text that explores a topic or event in a creative or humorous way
_____ :	A limitation that affects your writing
_____ :	The people who read your writing
_____ :	Clear communication and support of a main idea
_____ :	A brainstorming strategy for getting your ideas down on paper
_____ :	A stage of writing that involves making decisions, planning ideas, and identifying assignment guidelines
_____ :	A topic that you have made more specific by considering your purpose, audience, and constraints
_____ :	A text that gives the audience information about a topic
_____ :	A brainstorming strategy that helps you organize your thoughts
_____ :	A short piece of writing that focuses on one main idea
_____ :	A text that convinces its audience to adopt a belief or take an action
_____ :	A text that shares a personal experience or belief
_____ :	The goal of a text
_____ :	The focus of a writing assignment
_____ :	What you already know about a topic

Lesson 7.4
Writing a Thesis or Purpose Statement

OBJECTIVES
- ★ Recognize the characteristics of a good thesis statement.
- ★ Understand the difference between a thesis statement and a purpose statement.

BIG IDEA

Readers will know what to expect from your writing when you construct a well-written thesis statement or purpose statement. This statement will also give you a clear structure for your paper.

This lesson will discuss three steps in creating a thesis statement:

- Decide Between a Thesis and Purpose Statement
- Combine a Narrowed Topic and Controlling Idea
- Strengthen Your Thesis Statement

Decide Between a Thesis and Purpose Statement

Thesis statements and purpose statements are both _____, _____ previews of _____ pieces of writing.

Define the term **thesis statement**.

In what type of writing are thesis statements especially common?

Where do thesis statements almost always appear?

What do **purpose statements** announce and preview?

In what kind of reports are purpose statements most commonly found?

Where do purpose statements appear?

Combine a Narrowed Topic and Controlling Idea

The first step in creating a thesis statement is _____ so that you can choose a _____ _____.

Lesson 7.4 | Writing a Thesis or Purpose Statement

Define the term **controlling idea**.

When choosing a controlling idea, consider the _____ of your paper.

On Your Own

Read the following controlling ideas for the topic "student loan debt" and determine the purpose. Check the box next to your answer.

Student loan debt should be regulated by the government.

☐ Persuade
☐ Inform

Student loan debt is the subject of numerous proposed government reforms.

☐ Persuade
☐ Inform

Avoid using **hedging words** like *sometimes* or *kind of*, as they make your meaning seem _____.

To create a thesis statement, simply combine your _____ _____ and your _____ _____.

On Your Own

Practice creating your own thesis statements by combining narrowed topics and controlling ideas in the text boxes below.

Narrowed Topic	+	Controlling Idea
	+	
	+	

Strengthen Your Thesis Statement

To make your thesis statement stronger, consider adding _____ _____.

One way to strengthen a thesis would be to include the _____ for your _____. To create this type of thesis, add a **subordinating conjunction** like *because* or *including*; then, insert a brief _____ of your reasoning.

Example:
> Social media has changed the way people communicate with each other <u>because</u> of the ease with which friends can contact each other.

Lesson Wrap-up

Key Terms

Define the following Key Terms from this lesson.

Academic Writing:

Argument:

Audience:

Controlling Idea:

Drafting:

Hedging Word:

Informative Text:

Introduction:

Main Idea:

Narrowed Topic:

Paragraph:

Persuasive Text:

Pre-writing:

Purpose:

Purpose Statement:

Revising:

Subordinating Conjunction:

Thesis Statement:

Topic Sentence:

Lesson 7.5
Organizing and Outlining a Longer Paper

OBJECTIVE

★ Identify the characteristics and purposes of different types of **outlines**.

BIG IDEA

Organizing your writing will keep you from getting lost during the **writing process** and will keep your writing clear and easy to follow.

In this lesson, you will learn how to use three different types of **outlines**:

- Working Outline
- Topic Outline
- Sentence Outline

Define the term **outline.**

Working Outline

Working outlines are _____.

List the two important functions of a working outline:

1.

2.

What should you do if you find yourself moving in a slightly **different direction than you originally** planned?

Topic Outline

Topic outlines use short _____ to represent the
_____ of your paper.

Organizational Patterns

List the six organizational patterns:

1.   4.

2.   5.

3.   6.

© HAWKES LEARNING

Building the Outline

Fill in the topic outline below with your own ideas about adopting pets versus purchasing them.

I. Adopting pets
    A.
        1.
        2.
    B.
        1.
        2.

II. Purchasing pets
    C.
        1.
        2.
    D.
        1.
        2.

Sentence Outline

What are the similarities and differences between sentence outlines and topic outlines?

Lesson Wrap-up

Key Terms

Define the following Key Terms from this lesson.

Brainstorming:

Cause and Effect:

Chronological:

Compare and Contrast:

Drafting:

Entertaining Text:

Evidence:

Free-writing:

Grouping:

Heading:

Informative Text:

Order of Importance:

Organizational Pattern:

Outline:

Paragraph:

Persuasive Text:

Phrase:

Pre-writing:

Reflective Text:

Revising:

Sentence Outline:

Spatial:

Subheadings:

Supporting Detail:

Thesis Statement:

Topic Outline:

Topical:

Working Outline:

Writing Center:

Lesson 7.6
Writing with Technology

OBJECTIVES:

- ★ Identify and implement file organization strategies.
- ★ Identify and use shortcut keys.
- ★ Identify the best strategies for saving electronic documents.
- ★ Learn strategies for writing with technology.
- ★ Recognize proper use of spell-check.
- ★ Recognize the steps of page formatting.

BIG IDEA

Learning to utilize technology in an efficient way will help you avoid unexpected stress and save valuable time and energy when writing.

This lesson will discuss four important aspects of writing with technology:

- Saving Your Work
- Using Grammar and Spell-Check
- Formatting the Page
- Using Keyboard Shortcuts

Saving Your Work

When saving your work:

    Don't wait _____.

    Make a habit of saving your work every _____.

    Remind yourself with a _____.

    Consider saving your work in _____.

    Think about purchasing an _____.

Using Grammar and Spell-Check

Grammar and spell-check are useful, but they are not _____.

Spell-check should never replace _____ _____.

To enable grammar and spell-check in Microsoft Word:

1. Open _____

2. Select _____

© HAWKES LEARNING

3. In the pop-up box, select _____

4. Check _____

Formatting the Page

List the three common formatting options and a brief summary of each:

1.
2.
3.

Using Keyboard Shortcuts

Complete the following table with keyboard shortcuts. Keep the list handy until you get the hang of them.

Command	Windows	Mac
Save your work		
Undo your last action		
Highlight all text		
Cut highlighted text		
Copy highlighted text		
Paste cut/copied text		
Bold highlighted text		

Lesson Wrap-up

Key Terms

Define the following Key Terms from this lesson.

Editing:

Format:

Header:

Page Margin:

Page Number:

Lesson 7.7
Writing a First Draft

OBJECTIVE

★ Understand the importance of a first draft.

BIG IDEA

The first step in the drafting stage is to write your first draft. Having a set strategy will help you move more easily through the drafting process.

During the drafting stage, you should focus on _____ between your ideas. There's no pressure to produce an error-free paper. You can always **revise** and **edit** it later.

This lesson will teach you strategies for writing your first draft.

Preparation

To make sure that your writing time is productive, gather all of your _____ and _____ ahead of time.

You will need any _____ or mind maps you made during the pre-writing process as well as your finished _____ and research notes.

Your **workspace** can also play a big role in your ability to _____.

Writing

List the four recommendations you should keep in mind as you write:

1.

2.

3.

4.

Lesson Wrap-up

Test Yourself

Next to each statement, write **T** for True or **F** for False. Check your work using the Answer Key in the back of the book.

1. _____ Spelling and grammar are the main things to focus on when writing your first draft.

2. _____ You must write your introduction first and the conclusion last.

3. _____ You should have a large chunk of writing done by the time you start your first draft.

4. _____ If you get stuck on a sentence or paragraph, push yourself to keep moving forward.

5. _____ You should be clearly supporting your thesis statement in every paragraph.

6. _____ You shouldn't be adding supporting details in the drafting stage.

7. _____ Your workspace plays a big role in your ability to focus.

8. _____ Drafting is the last stage before you turn in your paper.

9. _____ Your first draft doesn't need to be perfect.

10. _____ You should review your outline before you start drafting.

Key Terms

Define the following Key Terms from this lesson.

Audience:

Conclusion:

Drafting:

Editing:

Introduction:

Outline:

Paragraph:

Revising:

Supporting Detail:

Thesis Statement:

Workspace:

Lesson 7.8
Using Paragraphs Effectively

OBJECTIVES

- ★ Recognize the use of different transition types.
- ★ Understand elements of an effective paragraph.
- ★ Understand the structure of a longer text.

BIG IDEA

A longer text follows a particular pattern similar to what you follow when writing one single paragraph: an introduction, body paragraphs which contain your main points, and a conclusion.

A good paragraph always includes a **topic sentence** that previews the _____ _____ of the paragraph. This idea is _____ by the information in the **support sentences**. Finally, the **concluding sentence** ties all of the information _____.

Complete the following diagram with the elements of a good paragraph:

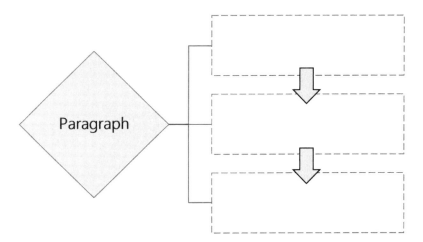

In this lesson, you will learn how to use three different types of paragraphs to build a longer text:
- Introductory Paragraphs
- Body Paragraphs
- Concluding Paragraphs

Introductory Paragraphs

Where do **introductory paragraphs** appear?

Lesson 7.8 | Using Paragraphs Effectively

What do introductory paragraphs do?

Often, authors begin the introduction with an interesting **fact** or **example** to get the audience _____ in the topic.

Step-by-Step Checklist: Introductions

- ✓ Start by _____
- ✓ Grab _____
- ✓ Give _____
- ✓ Help _____
- ✓ End _____

Write an example of a weak and strong introductory sentence for the topic "eating healthy."

Weak	
Strong	

Body Paragraphs

Body paragraphs contain the _____ _____ of your paper. They point back to your _____ _____ by sharing supporting details, or _____.

List the seven **supporting details** and a brief definition of each:

1.
2.
3.
4.
5.
6.
7.

The order of your body paragraphs depends on the _____ _____ of your paper. Follow your _____ to make sure that your paragraphs are organized in a logical, meaningful way.

Transition Paragraphs

Define the term **transitions**.

Transitions can be _____, _____, and even _____.

List two common transitions that show *order* and two that show *relationships*.

1.   1.

2.   2.

Concluding Paragraphs

Concluding paragraphs, or _____, help your audience reflect on the information you presented in your _____ _____.

Step-by-Step Checklist: Conclusions

- ✓ Begin _____
- ✓ Sum _____
- ✓ Explain _____
- ✓ Show _____
- ✓ Finally, _____

Lesson Wrap-up

Key Terms

Define the following Key Terms from this lesson.

Anecdote:

Audience:

Body Paragraphs:

Concluding Paragraph:

Concluding Sentence:

Conclusion:

Description:

Evidence:

Example:

Expert Analysis:

Fact:

Introduction:

Introductory Paragraph:

Main Idea:

Organizational Pattern:

Outline:

Paragraph:

Reflection:

Statistic:

Support Sentence:

Supporting Detail:

Thesis Statement:

Topic Sentence:

Transition:

Lesson 7.9
Revising a Longer Text

OBJECTIVE

★ Learn a process for revising a longer text.

BIG IDEA

Even after a first draft is complete, your writing still needs careful revision before it's ready for your audience. In this stage of the writing process, you will be looking for opportunities to improve content.

Revising is the time to improve your _____.

Once you have finished revising the ideas in the text, you can think about **editing** your sentences for _____, _____, and _____ errors.

In this lesson, you will learn how to revise the ideas in a longer text.

Revising Ideas

What two main areas does **revising** involve?

What questions should you ask yourself as you revise for *focus*?

1.
2.
3.
4
5.
6.

What questions should you ask yourself when revising for *development*?

1.
2.
3.
4
5.

Revision Strategies

List the guidelines that will help you revise more effectively:

Revise _____

Keep _____

Get _____

Take _____

Lesson Wrap-up

Key Terms

Define the following Key Terms from this lesson.

Academic Writing Process:

Audience:

Conclusion:

Development:

Drafting:

Editing:

Focus:

Introduction:

Main Idea:

Outline:

Paragraph:

Purpose:

Revising:

Supporting Detail:

Thesis Statement:

Topic Sentence:

Writing Center:

Lesson 7.10
Participating in Peer Review

OBJECTIVES

- ★ Identify constructive criticism.
- ★ Learn a process for participating in a peer review.
- ★ Recognize the importance of peer review.
- ★ Recognize the role of a peer reviewer.
- ★ Recognize the role of an author during a peer review.

BIG IDEA

Sharing your ideas and receiving advice from a classmate or other trusted peer helps you both improve your writing and broaden your perspective. Peer review is an important stage in the academic writing process that should not be ignored.

Define the term **peer review.**

In this lesson, you will learn how to get the most out of a peer review as both the author and the reviewer.

Author

List the four peer review steps you should take as an author and write a brief description of each:

1.

2.

3.

4

Reviewer

List the five characteristics to keep in mind as you give feedback and write a brief description of each:

1.

2.

3.

4

5.

© HAWKES LEARNING

Lesson 7.10 | Participating in Peer Review

What questions can you ask yourself as you read through the *introduction*?

- _____
- _____
- _____

What questions can you ask yourself as you read through the *body paragraphs*?

- _____
- _____
- _____
- _____
- _____

What questions can you ask yourself as you read through the *conclusion*?

- _____
- _____

Fill in the following table by re-writing the unhelpful criticism to be constructive, or helpful.

Unhelpful	Helpful
I don't like your introduction.	
How do you not know how to spell *experiment*?	
The paper's fine.	
I have no idea what you're trying to say.	

Lesson Wrap-up

Key Terms

Define the following Key Terms from this lesson.

Audience:

Body Paragraphs:

Conclusion:

Constructive Criticism:

Drafting:

Editing:

Evidence:

Introduction:

Main Idea:

Peer Review:

Revising:

Supporting Detail:

Thesis Statement:

Topic Sentence:

Lesson 7.11
Submitting a Longer Text

OBJECTIVES

- ★ Identify elements of MLA style.
- ★ Learn how to incorporate visuals into a longer text.
- ★ Recognize the importance of consistency in layout.
- ★ Understand how to submit a longer text.
- ★ Understand the differences between layout and design.

BIG IDEA

There are some formatting decisions you need to make before submitting the final version of your written work. This is an important step that should not be skipped.

In this lesson, you will learn three steps in submitting a longer text:

- Choose a Layout and Design
- Add Visuals
- Print or Upload Your Work

Choose a Layout and Design

Define the term **layout**.

Define the term **design**.

_____ often determines the _____ and _____ of your finished work.

Here are some basic rules and guidelines for MLA formatting:

- Research papers should include a **running head** half an inch from the _____ of the page, on the right-side _____ of each page. In your running head, include your _____ _____ followed by the _____ _____.

- Except for the _____ _____, all sides of your paper should have one-inch _____. The first line of each paragraph should be _____ by half an inch, and all of the text should be _____-_____.

What does the acronym ACE stand for?

A:

C:

E:

Add Visuals

Using visuals in a text helps you _____ your audience better and _____ your ideas more clearly.

Write a brief summary of the following guidelines you should consider when choosing visuals in your writing.

Think about your *purpose*:

Think about your *genre*:

Think about your *design:*

Print or Upload

The last step in _____ a text is actually printing or uploading the final copy.

Always schedule yourself _____ time in case of printer or computer _____.

You should also _____-_____ your work once it's been printed or published.

Lesson Wrap-up

Key Terms

Beside each definition, write the corresponding term.

_____: Colors, fonts, and images included in a text

Lesson 7.11 | Submitting a Longer Text

_____ : An acronym (Appealing, Consistent, Easy to read) for thinking about the layout and design of a text

_____ : The people who read your writing

_____ : A strategy that breaks up a writing assignment into five stages: pre-writing, drafting, revising, editing, and submitting

_____ : The size and style of letters

_____ : A text intended for instructors or students

_____ : A stage of writing that involves formatting a text and sharing it with its audience

_____ : The way text and images are arranged on a page or screen

_____ : The style and arrangement of a text

_____ : Working with another person in order to give feedback on each other's papers

_____ : The goal of an image

_____ : A type of writing

_____ : In an MLA paper, the page number and author's last name, which appear in the top-right corner of the document

Chapter 8
Research

Lesson 8.1
Researching and Writing Responsibly

OBJECTIVES

★ Recognize the characteristics of plagiarism.
★ Understand how to avoid plagiarism in writing.

BIG IDEA

You can use research to find sources of information that support your claim. You must give proper credit to the authors of the sources you use.

In this lesson, you will learn about the following:

- The Role of Sources in Research Writing
- Avoiding Plagiarism with Proper Documentation
- The Basics of Research Styles

Define the term **plagiarism**.

The Role of Sources in Research Writing

_____ can include many forms of texts—artwork, speeches, recordings, movies, articles, etc.—that provide _____ relevant to your particular goal.

In academic writing, _____ reliable sources is not only required, it's _____ if you want to establish yourself as a _____ writer.

Using research to explore the right sources has a number of advantages:

- _____ your opinion about a topic

- Offers powerful _____ to highlight your main arguments

- Adds _____ to your writing

- Provides _____ and _____ information

- _____ your audience where they can find further information

© HAWKES LEARNING

Integrating Source Information

List the three main ways to integrate sources into your writing:

1.

2.

3.

Summarizing

A **summary** is a _____ sentences that explain a _____ amount of information. Because summaries are _____, they should only be used when you need to _____ your **audience** about important _____ _____ on a topic.

Paraphrasing

When you **paraphrase**, you explain someone's _____ or _____ using _____ _____ _____. Paraphrases can explain a text's _____ or add _____ to the author's argument.

Quoting

Quotations are the _____ _____ of a source.

Quotes should be reserved for instances when the author's _____ is _____ or _____.

Avoiding Plagiarism with Proper Documentation

When you use _____ or _____ from an outside source without _____ the author, you commit _____.

If you don't _____ the source, or cite it _____, you are committing plagiarism.

Track your sources as you conduct your research.

To avoid accidental plagiarism, use a _____ or _____ _____ to keep track of your research. The key is to immediately _____ material you might use in your paper.

Avoiding Plagiarism with Proper Documentation

List the four source details you should record:

1.
2.
3.
4.

Use proper in-text citations.

Define the term **in-text citation**.

Define the term **signal phrase**.

Complete the following examples of signal phrases:

_____, "I don't expect to try to get people to like everything I do. I want them to respect what I do."

_____ that the majority of people who wear diamond jewelry are unaware of the consequences of mining for this rock.

If you do not identify the _____ _____ in the paragraph, include it in an _____-_____ _____ at the end.

Don't forget to include every source you use on the _____-_____ _____ or in the references list.

You must put *all* direct quotes in _____ _____.

In MLA style, direct quotes require an _____-_____ _____ that includes the _____ _____ where the quote was originally found.

If you are unable to fit the _____ _____ in the sentence itself, add the author's _____ _____ to the citation.

Checklist: Avoiding Plagiarism

- ✓ _____
- ✓ _____
- ✓ _____
- ✓ _____

The Basics of Research Styles

List the four most common formatting styles:

1.
2.

3.
4.

MLA

What does MLA stand for?

MLA recommends utilizing the "_____, _____, _____"
process, which requires you to *think* about what types of source are _____ to
your _____, *select* _____ sources and source
information, and *organize* your _____ in a clear manner.

List the nine MLA Core Elements of thorough and organized citations:

1.
2.
3.
4.
5.
6.
7.
8.
9.

APA

What does APA stand for?

APA papers strive to sound as _____ or _____ as possible.

Writers using APA style are expected to avoid _____-_____
_____ (like *I* and *me*), _____-_____
_____ (like *you* and *your*), _____, and _____.

Since APA style is often used for writing about _____ and _____, writers are asked to use the following guidelines when choosing their _____:

- Be as _____ as possible
- Be sensitive to _____ and unintentional _____
- Write about people as _____ participants, not _____ components

CMS

What does CMS stand for?

List the two options that CMS offers for citing research sources:

1.
2.

The Notes-and-Bibliography Method is preferred by the _____ because it allows for easily _____ sources and _____ additional information.

The Parentheses-and-Reference-List Method is preferred for _____ and _____ because it prioritizes the _____ _____ of sources.

CSE

What does CSE stand for?

List the three different methods that CSE uses for documenting sources:

1.
2.
3.

The citation-sequence system organizes sources according to the _____ that they _____ in the text.

In the citation-name system, each source is assigned a _____, which is used to refer to that source throughout the document. The _____ of sources at the end of the paper is

Lesson 8.1 | Researching and Writing Responsibly

_____ and _____ according to _____ order.

The name-year system uses _____-_____ _____ that include the _____ _____ of the author(s) as well as the source's _____ _____.

Lesson Wrap-up

Key Terms

Beside each definition, write the corresponding term.

_____: A list of sources at the end of an MLA-styled text

_____: A phrase used to identify source information—like the title and author—within a sentence

_____: Rewording the words of another person in order to explain the text's purpose or to add clarity to the author's argument

_____: The direct words of a source

_____: An opinion or statement shared by someone who is knowledgeable about a topic

_____: An argument or statement, usually supported by evidence

_____: A note in a paragraph that tells the reader which words and ideas come from a source

_____: The research style guide created by a group of scholars dedicated to research in modern languages

_____: A research style created by the Council of Science Editors

_____: The people who read your writing

_____: The research style guide created by psychologists used for academic documents such as journal articles and books

_____: A long example told as a story

_____: A research style guide published by the University of Chicago Press

_____: A way to help the audience find information in a text

Lesson Wrap-up

_____: The act of using borrowed words or ideas without giving credit to the author

_____: A pair of punctuation marks used to repeat someone else's words

_____: A set of standards used for research writing within a particular discipline

_____: The process of conducting research and using sources to compose arguments

_____: An original document or first-hand account that a writer consults for research

_____: A number or percentage that represents research data

_____: A few sentences that explain a large amount of information

Lesson 8.2
Making a Research Plan

OBJECTIVES

- ★ Create a research plan.
- ★ Evaluate research methods based on research purpose.
- ★ Recognize types of research.
- ★ Understand the characteristics of a credible writer.
- ★ Understand the importance of a research timeline.
- ★ Understand the importance of preliminary research.
- ★ Understand when to use field research.
- ★ Understand when to use online research.

BIG IDEA

Your research should play a meaningful role in the content and organization of your paper. Making a research plan will give you the direction and preparation you need to use research effectively.

In this lesson, you will learn to create a research plan in four steps:

- Consider Your Purpose and Guidelines
- Conduct Preliminary Research
- Think about Different Research Methods
- Schedule a Research Timeline

Consider Your Purpose and Guidelines

The first step in creating a research plan is identifying your _____. This determines what _____ your research should play in your writing.

When writing for work or school, you'll follow guidelines determined by your _____ or _____. You'll need to carefully review their instructions before deciding on the types of _____ to include.

Conduct Preliminary Research

Preliminary research will help you ensure that there is _____ material to _____ your _____ _____.

Two ways to conduct preliminary research:

    Use a _____ _____ like Google or Bing.

    Do a quick search of your library's _____.

Preliminary research is an excellent way to _____ _____ the main ideas in your paper.

Think about Different Research Methods

Library Catalogs and Databases

Academic journals contain _____ written by _____ or other _____ in a particular field.

Most libraries have an _____ _____ that you can use to search available materials.

You should also consider meeting with a _____ in person for assistance with your research.

Internet Searches

On the internet, you can find _____, _____ _____, _____, and _____.

Conducting online research is an excellent way to find source material on _____ _____ topics like _____ and _____ _____.

Because of the large amount of information available online, you must carefully _____ each source to be sure the information is _____.

Field Research

Field research involves personally collecting information through _____ and _____.

It's important to consider your assignment _____ just in case you need to _____ extra time to gather your research.

On Your Own

Identify different types of sources that could be used for each research purpose provided.

Purpose of Research	Types of Sources
To investigate the effects of a particular medicine on lung cancer	
To persuade the audience that chemical testing on animals should be stopped	

| To inform the audience of a typical student's perspective on a U.S. presidential race | |

Schedule a Research Timeline

Add scheduled _____ _____ to your **planner** so that you don't _____ or fall behind. Add any research _____ that your instructor has required.

List two examples of special situations that may require extra planning:

1.
2.

Lesson Wrap-up

Key Terms

Define the following Key Terms from this lesson.

Academic Journal:

Credibility:

Field Research:

Planner:

Pre-writing:

Writing Center:

Lesson 8.3
Organizing the Research Process

OBJECTIVE
★ Learn strategies for organizing the research process.

BIG IDEA

Organizing your research helps you find the source information you need in a timely way and prevents you from accidentally committing plagiarism.

In this lesson, you will learn how to organize your research using three helpful tools:
- Research Notes
- Research Journal
- Working Bibliography

Research Notes

Research notes are detailed _____ of the _____ information that you find during your research.

Instead of scanning through the _____ text every time you need to use a fact or statistic, you can use your _____ _____ to find the exact information you need.

Research notes also _____ you from losing _____ _____.

Research notes help you _____ your thoughts during the _____ _____.

Checklist: Research Notes

✓ _____

✓ _____

✓ _____

✓ _____

Lesson 8.3 | Organizing the Research Process

List two types of research notes that people commonly use:

1.

2.

On Your Own

Read the example paragraph below. Assume the text comes from a magazine for jobseekers. After you read the source text, read a paragraph that a student has written about the job search process. In the student's paragraph, identify the paraphrase that should have an in-text citation.

Source text:

> When searching for a job, it is vital to maintain a professional presence across all social media platforms. In other words, when you are in the midst of the job application process, any information you have put online could potentially be seen by a prospective employer. As such, you will want to refrain from posting inappropriate content on your social media profiles to avoid giving off an unprofessional and impolite image of yourself. This is not to say you should limit your own expression and creativity, but you should always be mindful of who might be looking at your posts when you are attempting to secure your dream job.

Student writing:

> If you are a college graduate looking for a job, it can feel overwhelming at times; however, there are a few tips and tricks that can help you secure a job if you are motivated. First, always carry a copy of your résumé on you if you think you might be introduced to a potential employer. Second, it is a good idea to clean up your social media presence as hiring managers and recruiters may visit your social media profiles to get an idea of what kind of candidate you are. Finally, dress to impress! Having a clean and professional appearance can go a long way when looking for a job.

Research Journal

A **research journal** is a _____ of your overall _____ _____.

You can use research journals to _____ your steps and find the source you need.

Working Bibliography

A **working bibliography** is a _____ _____ of sources that you plan to _____ in your _____.

Once you reach the _____ stage of the _____ process, you will turn this bibliography into the _____-_____ page of your paper.

Consider arranging your sources according to _____ to your topic.

Lesson Wrap-up

Key Terms

Beside each definition, write the corresponding term.

_____: A stage of writing that involves writing out ideas and support/concluding sentences

_____: Rewording the words of another person in order to explain the text's purpose or to add clarity to the author's argument

_____: The statement or argument that an author tries to communicate

_____: A specific instance or illustration that demonstrates a point

_____: A piece of information that most people generally agree to be true

_____: A few sentences that explain a large amount of information

_____: A tool developed during pre-writing that provides a visual of a paper's organization and ideas

_____: A detailed record of source information you find during your research

_____: The direct words of a source

_____: A page at the end of your research paper that includes full bibliographic citations of each source in your essay

_____: Learning information through pictures, shapes, and colors

_____: A strategy that breaks up a writing assignment into five stages: pre-writing, drafting, revising, editing, and submitting

_____: A record of the overall research process

_____: A running list of sources you plan to use in your paper

Lesson 8.4
Identifying Types of Sources

OBJECTIVES

★ Identify different types of sources.
★ Understand the differences between popular and scholarly sources.
★ Understand the differences between primary and secondary sources.

BIG IDEA

When you are researching, you will come across a wide variety of sources. Depending on your purpose and audience, some sources will be more appropriate than others.

In this lesson, you will learn to group sources into two main categories:

- Primary vs. Secondary
- Popular vs. Scholarly

Primary vs. Secondary

Primary Sources

Primary sources include _____ documents, _____-_____ accounts, _____, _____ findings, and _____ of _____.

All of these items are considered primary if they were _____ or _____ by the _____ source.

Primary sources allow you to get as _____ as possible to the _____ of information.

Secondary Sources

Secondary sources are documents that _____ information from a _____ source.

On Your Own

In the table below, fill in the missing primary and secondary sources based on the ones already entered.

Primary	Secondary
A commencement address by Bill Gates	An article written in a newspaper reviewing the commencement address

	A book review of *East of Eden* by John Steinbeck
A study on birth rates in Ecuador	
The Mayflower Compact	
	A biography of Oprah Winfrey
A survey of millennials who use Tinder	

If a source is too _____ from the original, it may be _____.

Secondary sources are useful when you don't have _____ to the _____ documents.

Popular vs. Scholarly

Popular Sources

A **popular source** is a document written for the _____ _____. The authors of these sources may or may not be _____ in their _____.

Complete the table below with an example for each type of popular source.

Type	Example
Books	
Magazines	
Movies	
Newspapers	
Websites	

Scholarly Sources

Scholarly sources are usually _____ _____ and contain articles that have been written by _____ and _____-_____ by other experts.

Define the term **research database**.

Lesson 8.4 | Identifying Types of Sources

You can access these databases through your college _____.

The _____ and _____ of your writing will determine if you should use _____ or _____ sources.

Lesson Wrap-up

Test Yourself

Next to each source, write **P** for Primary or **S** for Secondary. Check your work using the Answer Key in the back of the book

1. _____ Piano music written by Mozart

2. _____ Biography on Winston Churchill

3. _____ Article about John F. Kennedy's inaugural address

4. _____ *The Rights of Man* by Thomas Paine

5. _____ Website about Daniel Boone

Key Terms

Define the following Key Terms from this lesson.

Academic Journal:

Peer Review:

Popular Source:

Primary Source:

Research Database:

Scholarly Source:

Secondary Source:

Works Cited:

Lesson 8.5
Evaluating the Credibility of Sources

OBJECTIVE

★ Identify credible sources.

BIG IDEA

It's vital to use credible sources to support your claims so that your audience will be more likely to believe them.

This lesson will discuss four steps of identifying a credible research source:

- Look for Potential Bias in the Information
- Make Sure the Information is Relevant
- Check the Credentials of the Author or Organization
- Research the Credibility of Source Material

Look for Potential Bias in the Information

Bias is a term used to describe a person's _____ and _____.

A credible author will work to keep his or her writing as _____ and _____ as possible.

As you check for credibility, think about the author's _____. In a biased text, the author may have a _____ purpose that is different from the _____ purpose.

A research source can also contain _____ if the author is _____ with a particular organization or _____.

One final sign of bias is extremely _____ or _____ language.

Make Sure the Information is Relevant

The second step in evaluating the credibility of a source is checking for _____.

A relevant source will provide _____, _____ information about a topic.

Relevant sources are also _____.

Topics that _____ rapidly may require sources from the last _____ _____.

Lesson 8.5 | Evaluating the Credibility of Sources

What questions can you use to evaluate a source's relevance?

1.

2.

3.

Check the Credentials of the Author or Organization

The credibility of a research source can be affected by the author's _____ _____. An expert will have extensive _____ and _____ in a topic.

Sometimes, _____ experience in a topic is more important than _____ credentials.

Be aware of potential _____ of _____.

Give an example of a **conflict of interest**.

Research the Credibility of Source Material

A credible source will _____ other credible sources. Skim through any _____ _____ to make sure the information seems _____ and credible.

Any time an author uses information from other persons or organizations, that material must be _____ properly. If a text does not _____ a list of sources, the information may be _____ or _____.

Lesson Wrap-up

Test Yourself

Next to each source, write **C** for Credible or **N** for Not Credible. Check your work using the Answer Key in the back of the book.

1. _____ An article, written by a company that makes sunscreen, arguing that **sunscreen is the only real protection from skin cancer.**

2. _____ An article on a university website about the environmental impact of development on local species.

3. _____ A book written by a literature professor about the significance of character development in *The Adventures of Huckleberry Finn*.

4. _____ An article on an animal shelter's website about how owning an animal increases life expectancy.

5. _____ A blog post written by an unknown author that argues that hand-writing information helps you retain it longer.

Key Terms

Define the following Key Terms from this lesson.

Agenda:

Argument:

Audience:

Bias:

Conflict of Interest:

Credibility:

Development:

Focus:

Informative Text:

Paragraph:

Purpose:

Relevance:

Visual Learning:

Works-cited Page:

Lesson 8.6
Applying MLA Styles and Formatting

OBJECTIVE
- ★ Learn strategies for using research in a text.
- ★ Understand MLA guidelines for citing a research source.

BIG IDEA

MLA style is most commonly used in English and other humanities. Using these guidelines will strengthen your writing by helping you properly acknowledge your sources and format your papers consistently.

In this lesson, you will learn how to:
- Format Your Research Paper
- Integrate Borrowed Ideas
- Create a Works-Cited Page

Format Your Research Paper

List the settings for a page layout in MLA style:

1.
2.
3.
4.
5.
6.

Write the template for the **heading** that goes in the top left corner of the paper's first page:
-
-
-
-

Guidelines for formatting in-text elements:

Typically spell out numbers less than _____ _____ unless _____ used in the paper

Choose a consistent _____ _____ for the entire paper (either 12- or 24-hour)

Provide a person's _____ and _____ name when introducing them for the first time

Italicize _____ titles and titles of _____ _____; put the titles of _____ or _____ works in quotation marks

Integrate Borrowed Ideas

You must give credit to other authors using both _____-_____ _____ and a list of _____ _____.

Define the term **in-text citation**.

Define the term **works-cited page**.

To avoid **plagiarism**, you must use correct in-text citations for _____, _____, and _____ text. You can also use _____ _____ to introduce source information, like the _____ and _____, within a sentence.

Write an example of a **signal phrase**.

In-Text Citations

In-text citations provide source information in _____ at the end of a sentence. They follow an _____-_____ format.

Using the examples in the lesson, complete the following in-text citations.

- Citation with one author and single page ( )
- Citation with one author and multiple pages ( )
- Citation with two authors ( )
- Citation with two separate sources ( )
- Citation with three or more authors ( )

Summaries

Define the term **summary**.

Use summaries when your readers need a _____ _____ of a topic but not specific details.

Lesson 8.6 | Applying MLA Styles and Formatting

As long as you've already identified the author in a _____ phrase, simply include the _____ range in the in-text citation.

If you're summarizing the entire text, you do not need to include _____ _____ in the in-text citation. Instead, simply identify the _____ _____ of the _____ in a signal phrase or in-text citation.

Paraphrases

Define the term **paraphrase**.

Whenever you paraphrase information, make sure that the _____ is different from the _____ material. Simply changing one or two words is _____ _____.

On Your Own

Read the passage below and paraphrase it in the space provided.

> It is widely accepted that the most efficient way to travel quickly through space is via nuclear reactor technology. In 2045, just a mere decade ago, astronaut Malea Thompson became the first human to travel to the closest star outside of our solar system, Alpha Centauri A. Scientists still debate whether or not there is other intelligent life in our galaxy, but one thing is certain: we are quickly discovering better ways to traverse the stars. An answer to this age-old question may be just a light year's reach away (Lasky and Bennett 55).

Quotations

Define the term **quotation**.

Place the quoted words inside _____ _____ so that your audience knows where the quotation _____ and _____.

Always include an in-text citation _____ following the quote.

Define the term **block quote**.

Create a Works-Cited Page

The _____ page of your research paper should be a list of _____ _____. It should include _____ source you referenced in the body of your paper.

Formatting the Page

Header

Maintain the _____ _____ (with your _____ _____ and _____ _____) that appears through the rest of the document.

Heading

Enter the heading, "_____ _____," on the first line of the page. It should be _____ and _____ inch from the top of the page.

Add a _____ space between the heading and the _____ entry in your list.

Entries

_____-space and _____ each entry in your list. If a source doesn't have an _____, alphabetize according to the first letter of the _____.

_____-align the first line of each entry.

If the entry exceeds one line, the subsequent lines should be _____. This is called a _____ _____.

Lesson Wrap-up

Key Terms

Define the following Key Terms from this lesson.

Audience:

Block Quote:

Container:

Credibility:

Hanging Indent:

Heading:

In-text Citation:

Italics:

Main Idea:

MLA:

Page Header:

Paraphrase:

Parentheses:

Plagiarism:

Quotation:

Quotation Marks:

Signal Phrase:

Summary:

Works-cited Page:

Answer Key

Chapter 1

1.2 Determining Your Personal Learning Styles

TEST YOURSELF
1. T
2. F
3. T
4. T
5. F
6. F
7. T
8. T
9. F
10. ACTIVE
11. INTUITIVE
12. SEQUENTIAL

1.3 Understanding and Reducing Stress

TEST YOURSELF
1. F
2. T
3. F
4. F
5. T
6. T
7. T
8. External
9. Internal
10. Semester exam

1.4 Keeping Yourself Organized

TEST YOURSELF
1. F
2. F
3. F
4. T
5. T
6. T
7. T
8. T
9. F
10. T

1.5 Managing Your Time Effectively

TEST YOURSELF
1. T
2. F
3. T
4. F
5. F
6. 10 hours with friends
7. At least 6 hours studying
8. 24 hours of studying
9. Top-down strategy
10. 2 hours
11. No
12. Multitasking

1.6 Taking Notes and Annotating Texts

TEST YOURSELF
1. F
2. T
3. T
4. F
5. F (Cornell notes)
6. T
7. F
8. T
9. 1 time
10. What you already know about a topic

1.7 Using Effective Study Strategies

TEST YOURSELF
1. F
2. T
3. F
4. F
5. T
6. F
7. F
8. T
9. T
10. T
11. F
12. T

1.8 Reducing Test Anxiety

TEST YOURSELF
1. F
2. T
3. T
4. T
5. F
6. T
7. F
8. T
9. T
10. F

1.9 Taking Advantage of Campus Resources

TEST YOURSELF
1. Student Services
2. The Library
3. Disabilities Services
4. Student Services
5. The Writing Center
6. The Academic Success Center
7. The Library
8. The Writing Center
9. The Library
10. 10. Disabilities Services

Chapter 2

2.3 Reading Actively and Purposefully

TEST YOURSELF
1. N
2. Y
3. Y

2.5 Identifying Organizational Patterns

TEST YOURSELF
a. 3
b. 5
c. 1
d. 2
e. 4

2.6 Using Context for Unfamiliar Words and Phrases

TEST YOURSELF
1. sad (answers will vary)
2. antonym
3. scared (answers will vary)
4. example
5. unlike

Chapter 3

3.1 Identifying Purpose and Tone

TEST YOURSELF
1. E
2. I
3. E
4. P
5. R
6. I
7. T
8. F
9. T
10. T

3.2 Analyzing Argumentation Strategies

TEST YOURSELF
1. L
2. E
3. P
4. E
5. L
6. P

Chapter 4

4.1 Understanding Nouns

GRAMMAR PRACTICE 1
- One lucky student will win this awesome bike. (Student = subject)
- My sister always gets good grades. (Sister = subject)

GRAMMAR PRACTICE 2
- The chicken ate a bug. ((bug = direct object)
- The farmer planted his crops. (crops = direct object)

GRAMMAR PRACTICE 3
- My nephew hid under the table and wanted me to find him. (object of the preposition = table)
- We went down the river and swam in the deep water. (objects of the prepositions = river, water)

GRAMMAR PRACTICE 4
- The mail truck has arrived! (adjective = mail)
- I can't believe the cat knocked over his own food bowl. (adjective = food)

4.2 Understanding Pronouns

GRAMMAR PRACTICE 1
- After soccer practice, I made sure to drink plenty of water.
- You aren't really a true Jacksonville Jaguars fan unless you get upset when they lose!

GRAMMAR PRACTICE 2
Singular Pronouns
- I was in the middle of cooking steak and potatoes when my friend invited me out to dinner.

Personal Pronouns
- The group decided that we would go for a walk after dinner; our stomachs needed help digesting.

GRAMMAR PRACTICE 3

First-person	Second-person	Third-person
What is up with me these days? I have been so scatterbrained lately that my friends are concerned.	What are your plans later on today? If you would like, we can go shopping.	She has been doing such a great job at work that they have promoted her to manager.

GRAMMAR PRACTICE 4
1. His
2. Her
3. Their

GRAMMAR PRACTICE 5
Answers will vary.

GRAMMAR PRACTICE 6
- At the time of the election, many people were unhappy with both candidates, which led to political unrest.

TEST YOURSELF
1. I (subjective), my (possessive)
2. They (subjective), you (objective), me (objective)
3. You (subjective), their (possessive)
4. My (possessive), that (relative)
5. Whomever (indefinite)

4.3 Understanding Verbs

GRAMMAR PRACTICE 1
- will
- am

4.4 Understanding Adjectives and Adverbs

GRAMMAR PRACTICE 1
- The elderly man limped painfully after his surgery.
- I shop at that store often.
- Mom hid her jewelry carefully.

4.5 Understanding Prepositions

GRAMMAR PRACTICE 1
Answers will vary.

4.6 Understanding Clauses and Conjunctions

TEST YOURSELF
1. I wanted ham, but we didn't have any, so we went out to eat instead.
2. We had ice cream and cake at the birthday party, but not everybody wanted some.
3. He and I will be getting married next year, so we have started planning now.
4. Ever since I started exercising, I have felt a lot better.
5. After snacking all day, I couldn't eat dinner.
6. In spite of our differences, we have remained friends since first grade.
7. We went over the mountain and through the woods.
8. I went through the yard and into the house.

4.7 Identifying the Characteristics of Sentences

TEST YOURSELF
- Whenever the four of us go shopping, I always spend too much money (period)
- Did you know the man down the street who passed away (question mark)
- Marcus and Steve joined our group and helped us raise money (period)
- Every time you get behind the wheel of a car, put your seatbelt on (period)
- Ever since I first saw you, I have thought you looked like Steve Carrell (period)

4.9 Using Consistent Subjects and Verbs

GRAMMAR PRACTICE 1
- Nothing you say will ever change my mind.
- Somebody rang my doorbell at 3:00 a.m.

GRAMMAR PRACTICE 2
The residents of that beautiful villa (**have**/has) left for the winter.
- Prepositional phrases: of that beautiful villa; for the winter
- Subject: residents
- Verb: have left

The houses in the path of the hurricane (was/**were**) destroyed.
- Prepositional phrases: in the path, of the hurricane
- Subject: houses
- Verb: were destroyed

4.12 Using Commas

GRAMMAR PRACTICE 1
- I bought a tent, sleeping bag, air mattress, and hiking boots.
- To get ready for the holiday season, the grocery store manager had to order extra ham, flour, sugar, cranberry sauce, green beans, and pumpkin pies.
- In preparing for her trip, Laura packed shampoo, conditioner, deodorant, her passport, her pillow, and a map of the city.

TEST YOURSELF
1. Finally,
2. Additionally,
3. After the train passed,
4. By that time,
5. Even though I was tired,
6. Although my sister was younger than I,
7. Excuse me,

4.13 Using Semicolons and Colons

TEST YOURSELF
1. My professor made the following statement:
2. I was sick today; I stayed home in bed.
3. When I was a child,
4. Every time I smell a certain odor,
5. For this art class, you will need a portfolio, colored pencils, drawing paper, and a sketching pencil.

4.14 Using Apostrophes

GRAMMAR PRACTICE 1
- Mark's car
- Jane's house
- Yesterday's newspaper
- Couple's marriage license
- Patients' symptoms

TEST YOURSELF
1. I'm; let's
2. She's
3. '80s
4. Cousins'
5. Children's

4.20 Spelling Commonly Confused Words

TEST YOURSELF
1. accept
2. affect
3. its
4. past
5. loose
6. choose
7. than
8. there
9. They're
10. too
11. to
12. weather
13. whose
14. You're
15. between
16. come
17. fewer
18. lie

Chapter 5

5.1 Determining a Writing Style

TEST YOURSELF
1. F
2. F
3. F
4. I
5. F
6. I
7. I
8. F

5.2 Using an Appropriate Tone

TEST YOURSELF
1. B
2. C
3. B
4. A
5. B
6. A
7. B
8. A
9. C
10. A
11. C
12. B
13. B

5.8 Emphasizing Words or Phrases

TEST YOURSELF
- Even though you have been busy, you still should've called me.
- Twirling gracefully in the fall breeze, the leaves reminded me of little ballerinas.
- After careful consideration, I have decided not to take the job in London.
- Whenever my mother-in-law comes around, I feel like I have been judged on my child rearing and my housekeeping.
- The position of lead scientist will be given to the employee who has shown the most dedication to this company.

Chapter 6

6.1 The Writing Process for Paragraphs

TEST YOURSELF
1. F
2. T
3. F
4. F
5. T
6. F
7. F
8. F
9. T
10. T

Chapter 7

7.2 Understanding Genre and Purpose

TEST YOURSELF
1. I
2. F
3. F
4. I
5. F

7.7 Writing a First Draft

TEST YOURSELF
1. F
2. F
3. T
4. T
5. T
6. F
7. T
8. F
9. T
10. T

Chapter 8

8.4 Identifying Types of Sources

TEST YOURSELF
1. P
2. S
3. S
4. P
5. S

8.5 Evaluating the Credibility of Sources

TEST YOURSELF
1. N
2. C
3. C
4. N
5. N

Notes

Notes

Notes

Notes

Notes

Notes

Notes

Notes